Niobrara County
High School
Library

ENCYCLOPEDIA OF GOOD HEALTH

MAINTAINING GOOD HEALTH

ENCYCLOPEDIA GOOD of OOD HEALTH

MAINTAINING GOOD HEALTH

Series Editors
MARIO ORLANDI, Ph.D., M.P.H.
and
DONALD PRUE, Ph.D.

Text by
TRISHA THOMPSON

Facts On File Publications
New York • Oxford

A FRIEDMAN GROUP BOOK

First published in 1989 by Facts On File Publications, Inc.
460 Park Avenue South
New York, New York 10016

Library of Congress Cataloging-in-Publication Data

Thompson, Trisha
Maintaining good health.

(Encyclopedia of good health)
Includes index.
1. Accidents—Prevention—Juvenile literature. 2. Safety education—Juvenile literature. 3. Medicine, Preventive—Juvenile literature. 4. Child abuse—Prevention—Juvenile literature. I. Title. II. Series: Spence, Annette. Encyclopedia of good health.
HV675.5.S64   1988   613.6   87-22142
ISBN 0-8160-1667-4

British CIP data available upon request

ENCYCLOPEDIA OF GOOD HEALTH: MAINTAINING GOOD HEALTH
was prepared and produced by
Michael Friedman Publishing Group, Inc.
15 West 26th Street
New York, New York 10010

Designer: Rod Gonzalez
Art Director: Mary Moriarty
Illustrations: Kenneth Spengler

Typeset by BPE Graphics, Inc.
Color separated, printed, and bound in Hong Kong by South Seas International Press Company Ltd.

1 3 5 7 9 10 8 6 4 2

About the Series Editors

Mario Orlandi is chief of the Division of Health Promotion Research of the American Health Foundation. He has a Ph.D. in psychology with further study in health promotion. He has written and edited numerous books and articles, among them The American Health Foundation Guide to Lifespan Health *(Dodd Mead, 1984), and has received numerous grants, awards, and commendations. Orlandi lives in New York City.*

Dr. Donald M. Prue is a management consultant specializing in productivity improvement and wellness programs in business and industrial settings. He was formerly a senior scientist at the American Health Foundation and holds a doctorate in clinical psychology. He has published over forty articles and books on health promotion and was recognized in the Congressional Record *for his work. Prue lives in Houston, Texas.*

About the Author

Trisha Thompson has been a writer and editor in the health field for the past seven years, with articles appearing in various publications such as Fame, American Baby, Weight Watcher's Magazine, Grandparents Today, *and* Esquire. *She has also written scripts for the American Baby Cable TV show. Thompson lives in Shutesbury, Massachusetts.*

C O N T

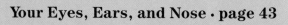

How to Use
This Book

Maintaining Good Health is part of a six-volume encyclopedia series of books on health topics significant to junior-high students. These health topics are closely related to each other, and, for this reason, you'll see references to the other volumes in the series appearing throughout the book. You'll also see references to the other pages *within* this book. These references are important because they tell you where you can find more interrelated and interesting information on the specific subject at hand.

Like each of the books in the series, this book is divided into two sections. The first section, "Head-To-Toe Body Maintenance," includes information on how to keep yourself well both mentally and physically. The second section, "Get Well, Stay Well," tells you how to make yourself well when you're sick and how to handle minor accidents. It's your responsibility to take advantage of this information and apply it to your life. Even though this book was written expressly for you and other people your age, you are the one who's in control of learning from it and thereby exercising good health habits for the rest of your life.

Head-To-Toe Body Maintenance

What Does Maintaining Good Health Mean? It means feeling, thinking, and looking your best. It involves taking responsibility for your own physical, mental, and emotional health. But in order to maintain good health, you need to know what actions to take to keep or get yourself well.

You also need to realize that you have the power to feel and look your best. Other people—parents, teachers, doctors—are there to help you. But nobody else can do your eating, exercising, cleansing, thinking, breathing, and coping for you. When you were a child, other people did many of these things for you, but not anymore. You may not yet be an adult, but you are no longer a child, and right now is the time to start making decisions concerning your health. The decisions you make now will affect you for the rest of your life.

This sounds like a lot of responsibility, doesn't it? Well, it is, but it's not as burdensome as it might seem. There are many things in life you will not be able to control, so take comfort in knowing that you do have a lot of control over your health and the way you feel. Learning how to keep yourself feeling good is an exhilarating experience because it gives you the power to make your life healthy.

Your Mind

This book begins with a look at the mental and emotional part of your health. We've chosen to discuss this important facet of your health here for two reasons. First, the way you feel about yourself, the way you perceive what others feel about you, and the way you interact with the world emotionally has an important and constant effect on your physical health. For instance, if you think you are tired, chances are you'll carry yourself as if you are tired and others will think you are tired.

Second, the brain is traditionally where most people think their emotions are centered. However, it is important for you to understand that you feel with your whole body, throughout the elaborate network of your nervous system. So, though we talk about mental health coming from your brain, you should also think about your thoughts and emotions as coming from throughout your body.

Everything you feel physically, you react to mentally and emotionally. For instance, when you touch the stove, you think "Hot! I must move my hand!" On the other hand, any emotion you feel, you can express physically. For instance, you may not really think that you are nervous about the party you are going to, but you can't keep your foot still while your dad is driving you over. All of these reactions—mental, emotional, and physical—make up your mental health. For more information, see "Stress and Mental Health."

Mental Health

Who is normal and who is not? Who is sane and who is insane? And if you're sane, are you mentally healthy?

Normality and abnormality are tricky things to judge, partly because at any given time and place, people are redefining what these words mean. What is considered normal today might have been considered abnormal as recently as a century ago. What is sane to a Muslim farmer might be crazy to a New York City cop.

Normality is also difficult to judge because it's not one single way of being, and it's not the same for every person. The different states of normal and abnormal mental health are charted along something called a *mental health continuum*. In the middle is average mental health, at one end is poor mental health, and at the other end is optimal (the best possible) mental health. In between these three points on the spectrum are varying degrees of mental wellness and mental illness.

Everyone goes through times when they feel more and less mentally healthy. This is perfectly normal, especially during adolescence, when you might often find yourself questioning who you are and what you think. All of us, no matter where we fall on the mental health continuum, strive to move closer and closer to optimal wellness.

There are specific ways to do this. You can begin by first understanding what the qualities of optimal mental health are so that you know what you're striving for. In the 1960s, a psychologist named Abraham Maslow came up with a list of qualities or characteristics that mentally healthy people seem to share. After more than twenty years, Maslow's list is still useful today. It has survived because it doesn't hold to the conventions of only one culture, and it allows for a lot of individuality and uniqueness in people. Here, then, are Maslow's ten qualities of mental health and what they can mean in your life.

A discussion of mental health may conjure up old-fashioned images of ''crazies'' in asylums. It needn't. For most of us, thinking about mental and emotional well-being means striving to go from average to optimal health.

ental Health Q and A

Q: What is the difference between a psychiatrist and a psychologist?

A: A psychiatrist is a person with a medical degree specializing in conditions that affect the mind, behavior, and the emotions. A psychologist is a specially trained person, usually not a physician, who studies behavior and conscious life and counsels people about their problems.

Q: What are emotions?

A: Emotions are the feelings you have about the things that happen to you everyday. They include love, fear, hate, happiness, and many other reactions.

Q: What is a nervous breakdown?

A: A nervous breakdown is a very general term referring to any mental disorder.

Q: What are some mental disorders?

A: Anxiety Neurosis—a constant state of concern and worry about what might happen in your life—to the point that everyday activities are inhibited.

Neuroasthenia—a condition where one feels unusually exhausted after only a little bit of activity.

Claustrophobia—a fear of closed-in spaces, such as elevators, underground garages, or tunnels.

Agoraphobia—a fear of open spaces. Agoraphobics find it difficult to be outside because they feel that so many bad things could happen to them there.

Depression—low spirits or a gloomy outlook, to the point that the sufferer doesn't want to do anything. Everyone gets depressed now and then. It becomes a serious mental disorder when it continues for a long time or when ordinary routine and responsibilities are neglected.

Schizophrenia—a severe condition that involves disturbances in thinking, a lack of understanding of reality, and a split between thoughts, actions, and emotions. Schizophrenics have a hard time interacting with others because they are unable to express their feelings and emotions. There is much that is not understood about schizophrenia, including its cause.

ADVICE? Listen to Your Own Common Sense First

An important factor to keep in mind when asking others, particularly your friends, for advice is that their suggestions come from their own perspectives, which may not be the same as yours. A good rule of thumb on taking advice: If your own common sense tells you something is wrong with the suggestion, it probably *doesn't* make sense for you. Get another, more knowledgeable opinion.

1. *Being "real."* This means having a genuineness that comes from being unselfconscious, at least most of the time. Being real is also known as being "down-to-earth." People who are real are comfortable with who they are, and they usually make others around them feel comfortable too.

People who are "unreal" are often called fake or phony or pretentious. These people aren't comfortable with themselves and so they're constantly trying to be another way. They put on different "masks" that they think will appear better to others and even to themselves.

Real people can and will tell you honestly how they feel about an issue even if it makes them appear silly or unpopular. Unreal people sometimes can't, sometimes just won't, speak honestly. They may tell you what they think you want

to hear or what they think most people would tell you. They may not be lying, they may be such strangers to themselves that *they* don't even know what they really think. Real people speak directly and openly. Unreal people often speak in a fearful, coded way that doesn't really say much of anything. Unreal people often are envious of what other people have and strive to "keep up with the Joneses." Real people are not threatened by others' fortunes; they have their own set of priorities and values.

2. *Being realistic.* Recognizing and accepting the world and people for what they are and not for what they should be is the second of Maslow's mental health qualities. This is a tough one for most of us. The world, people, and life often seem to be unfair, and it's sometimes very hard to avoid

Learning to accept and value people for who they are, faults and all, is one of life's hardest lessons. Your relationship with a close friend is a good place to start.

spending a lot of energy pushing against the way you feel things "shouldn't" be and prodding to get things to the way you feel they "should" be. The fact is, "shoulds" and "shouldn'ts" are not always important. There are things about the world and people that simply are, whether we think they ought to be or not.

This doesn't mean that it's always useless to try to correct what you see as an injustice. If that were true, slavery would never have been abolished, Nazis would rule the world, and your younger brother would always get away with telling lies about things you've done to him. Some wrongs should and can be righted.

What "being realistic" does mean is this: Repeatedly butting your head against a wall over something you can't and probably were not meant to change is not helpful or healthy. If you have a friend who is generally a good friend but occasionally acts in inconsiderate ways, constantly expecting her to change and become the considerate person you want her to be isn't helpful for you, your friend, or your friendship. If this quality in her bothers you so much, you need to rethink your friendship and decide whether her other good qualities make up for the bad ones. If not, you should dissolve the friendship. If so, you should try to expect from your friend what she

Sometimes only an objective party—a therapist, counselor, or religious advisor—can help solve a family problem. If this is the case in your family, take the initiative and suggest you get help as a group.

has taught you to expect, and not what you would *like* to expect. You cannot change people simply because you want to. They have to want to change themselves.

3. *Knowing your needs and satisfying them.* To be happy, to be satisfied with yourself, to be able to choose a career, a mate, a path in life, you must first know what your needs are and then how to meet them.

The meeting of people's needs is an important part of most relationships. In your family life, in school or work, and in love relationships and friendships, everyone involved wants to satisfy their needs. Your parents probably decided to

have children because they felt a need to nurture and love. You need your parents to help guide and support you. You need your brothers and sisters, and they need you, for guidance and friendship and, also, for learning how to share and get along with people. You need your teachers (whether you think so or not) to help you learn; your teachers need you in order to fulfill their desire to teach. You and your friends need one another for talking, sharing feelings and secrets, and having fun together. And in a love relationship, you and your boy- or girlfriend need each other for emotional and physical closeness, for experimenting with getting along with someone in a way that is

very different from getting along with your friends or your sister or brother.

These are all perfectly healthy needs. Unhealthy needs are needs that don't foster your growth as a person but, instead, stunt your growth or hurt other people—things like needing to win every basketball game in order to feel like a winner; needing to cheat from your best friend during weekly science exams; needing to get your older sister in trouble with your parents so you can feel like they love *you* most. Unhealthy needs often stem from healthy desires to feel confident, to succeed, and to feel loved. Instead of looking inside themselves to fulfill these basic needs (by believing in their abilities, by loving themselves), people sometimes look to others to do the fulfill-

ing for them. This never works out. Although other people in your life can and should help you satisfy some of your needs, other people cannot satisfy all of them.

4. *Taking responsibility for your own feelings and actions.* This means being able to say to your younger brother after you've snapped at him, "I'm sorry for yelling at you. I've had a hard day and I'm feeling tired and impatient." At the time, it may seem like your brother is trying to drive you crazy, but if you stop and think about why you're reacting so angrily, chances are you'll see that your feelings have little or nothing to do with your brother's behavior.

Of all the qualities of mental health, taking responsibility may have the most to do with ma-

People used to believe that the mentally ill were dangerous, to themselves and to others, and had to be kept away from society. Today, mentally ill people are treated humanely and live in surroundings designed to help them get well. We have realized that it is often good therapy for the patients to interact freely with others in the hospital.

© North Wind Picture Archives

turity. It takes maturity to know and be able to express your feelings and to take responsibility for your actions. It requires some growing up to know that taking responsibility for your feelings and actions will not make you seem like a bad person, but actually a better person.

5. *Being a free and autonomous person.* This may sound vague and strange to you, but all it means is listening to your own inner voice and acting on it instead of relying on the voices around you for direction. People who are autonomous (independent) are sensitive to their own feelings and desires. When they act, it's because they have chosen to act in a particular way. When people who aren't autonomous do something, it is often because they've let themselves be pres-

sured by others to act that way.

Image is very important to teenagers, and teens often make severe judgments of each other on the basis of image alone. It's tough to resist keeping up the image your friends keep up, even when you think that image may be dumb. This is because it's risky to be different, to speak the truth and openly admit your feelings. Your friends may call you a jerk for doing so. What you have to ask yourself is: Who is it more important for me to listen to—my friends or myself? People who are autonomous, or inner-directed, listen to themselves first. They care about other people, but they don't base their opinions of themselves on what others think.

Edward Lettau/FPG International

Fear of the unknown—each one of us has experienced it at various times. The trick is to not let it paralyze you—to take actions wisely and view what lies ahead as opportunity.

6. *Having a good self-image.* This means carrying in your mind an accurate and positive picture of who you are. This doesn't mean being conceited. In fact, a good self-image implies a realistic self-image, and being realistic means knowing your faults as well as your good points.

Recognizing your bad points is good. Trying to improve on them is better. Criticizing yourself for them is stupid. We all have our rotten sides; we wouldn't be human if we didn't. So just wipe the idea of "I must be a terrible person if I have this terrible quality" right out of your head. If you can't forgive yourself for the quirks that make you you, who can? Not passing judgment on yourself, trying to improve yourself, but not kicking yourself in the head for your imperfections, and giving yourself credit for your wonderful qualities enable you to develop a healthy self-image.

7. *Being comfortable with being alone and with silence.* People who are mentally and emotionally healthy are content to sometimes have only themselves as company. They enjoy peace and quiet. Wanting only to be alone isn't healthy either. The goal here is to strike a balance, and this is true in virtually every aspect of life. Being with people some of the time and being alone some of the time is healthy because it helps you achieve a kind of harmony. Always being with other people can serve as a way of escaping yourself and your problems. In that case, you are choosing to avoid yourself.

Even if your school or work schedule doesn't allow you much time to yourself, you should make a point of being alone for at least a portion of your waking hours, just to think or meditate (see page 80, "Meditation") or, simply, *be* by yourself. You'll most likely find that it's a good way to get to know yourself better and enjoy the person you are. It will make you want to return to the world of other people, renewed and refreshed. It will also give you confidence to get through lonely times in your life.

8. *Being capable of physical and emotional intimacy.* Opening yourself to others is frightening because when you do, you run the risk of being hurt or rejected. Not opening yourself to others will prevent you from feeling the pain of rejection, but it will also prevent you from feeling the intense happiness that can come from taking this risk.

Adolescence is the time when most people learn that intimacy with others *is* a risk, that it can cause pain as well as joy. Still, in either case, having close relationships usually gives you the opportunity to grow as a person.

9. *Being aware of your feelings and being able to express them in appropriate ways.* This doesn't mean being a phony and it doesn't mean being obnoxious. It means expressing your feelings in healthy ways—not through violence.

Being aware of your feelings doesn't always mean expressing them. Every situation is different, and you have to judge how, when, and whether to tell someone else how you feel about something. If you resent your best friend for having more spending money than you, it doesn't necessarily mean you should tell him or her about it. If you do decide to talk to him, you should do so in a positive way. Talk to your friend about how the two of you can make the financial differences between you less of a problem. Maybe you can agree to do more things together that don't require much money. The idea is to understand your feelings and deal with them in ways that will be good for you and the people involved.

Unfortunately, what happens more often in our culture is that people never even acknowledge their unpleasant feelings, and, when they do, they often go without expressing them in any way for years or perhaps their whole lifetime. Confronting problems is never fun but is definitely necessary for emotional well-being.

10. *Being a fully functioning person.* This means the highest sense of functioning—not just walking, talking, working, and breathing but living to your fullest potential. It means being comfortable with yourself. It means being open to new experiences, unafraid of the unknown, and even attracted to it. It means being hopeful about the future.

Fully functioning, or fulfilled, people are able to be creative, and this isn't limited to artists, writers, and musicians. Creativity can be expressed in many other ways—in the way you make a sandwich or put together an outfit, for example. As Abraham Maslow, the creator of this list, pointed out, "A first-rate soup is more creative than a second-rate painting." After all, a pot of soup could be as much an expression of creativity as an oil painting on a canvas. Part of being fully functioning means knowing that although others will set themselves up to judge who and what is first- or second-rate, *you* are your most important evaluator. If you try to do your best at least most of the time, that is what really matters and what will help you to become fulfilled. You don't have to try harder to become fully-functioning; you simply have to be yourself.

The History of Hair

Men's and women's hairstyles have changed as much as clothing styles have changed over the centuries—and that's a lot! Here is a brief lesson in the history (and hair-story) of hairstyles.

3,000 B.C. During these ancient days, Egyptian women used hairpins to curl their hair (archaeologists have even found hairpins and combs that date back to prehistoric times) and made long black wigs from sheep's wool or human hair. Sometimes they dyed stripes into the wigs for decoration, a style punk rockers would revive thousands of years later.

500 B.C. Greek men and women both wore their hair in knots at the top of their head. They also wore wigs, and about a hundred years later, Greek men began wearing their hair short. Romans were fond of wigs, especially blond wigs imported from Germany. Roman women dyed their hair and even sprinkled it with gold dust.

500 A.D. to 1400s. The Middle Ages were probably the dullest period of history as far as hairstyling is concerned. Men generally wore their hair short, and women tended to cover up their hair as a sign of modesty.

1400 to 1600. The Renaissance period, famous for advances in art and culture, brought renewed interest to hairstyling as well. Women used pearls, jewels, pieces of fabric, and braids to adorn their upswept and curled hairstyles.

1700s to 1900. France's King Louis XIV may have been history's first man to have a great impact on hairstyles. He and his court of wealthy and powerful aristocrats wore long, often powdered, curly wigs, and the fashion caught on.

The *pompadour* was the style of choice for women. Hair was swept straight up from the forehead and was often decorated with feathers, flowers, and even model ships. The styles were popular in the American colonies too, where men wore powdered wigs and women wore styles based on the French pompadour.

The French Revolution of 1789 brought about a dislike for anything associated with the overthrown aristocracy, and so hairstyles then tended to be short, plain, and left free. During the 1800s the *chignon* style, with its smooth knot of hair at the back of the head, became an instant classic, and women began getting waves ironed into their hair.

1920s to 1980s. The permanent wave, or "perm," which allowed women with stick-straight hair to have wavy locks even after many washings, was the rage in the early twenties—and, in different formulas, continues to be popular today. In the 1920s, the age of the boyish flapper style, short hairstyles for women became popular after a couple of celebrities made a chin-length haircut called the *bob* a hit. From the 1930s up to the 1950s, longer, waved hair for women was in. Short hair made a return in the fifties with styles such as the *pixie* and the *poodle.* The *French twist* and the *beehive* were also popular.

Men's hairstyles during the fifties remained more or less short and neat, with the most extreme style being the carpetlike *crewcut.* Then came the 1960s and the hippie movement. Men returned to the styles of their ancestors and grew their hair long. Shoulder-length hair, loose or in a ponytail, became the norm for teenagers and young adults, both male and female. For older women, wigs came back into style, and the *bouffant* hairdo was the rage.

Straight, long hair was the popular style of the 1970s, and during this decade men began using hairsprays, blow dryers, and perms to style their hair. British punk-music enthusiasts of the late 1970s and early 1980s had a big effect on hair (and clothing) styles. Soon, American teenagers were getting their hair cut and styled into stand-up spikes with brightly colored stripes dyed into them, just as the Egyptians did centuries before.

© R. Herzog/FPG International

© Grace Davies/Envision

Think twice about damaging your hair for the sake of style. Overdried, over-moussed, over-teased, hair rarely looks good even when it's coiffed in the style of the moment.

Help keep your hair silky and tangle-free at the beach by running a little conditioner through wet hair with a wide-toothed comb and then fastening it into a braid.

© Steve Smith/Wheeler Pictures

Your Hair, Scalp, and Skin

Hair, There, and Everywhere

It's too curly. It's too straight. It's too thin. It's too thick. It's too fine. It's too kinky. Considering that it's just a bunch of dead cells, hair gets a lot of attention and causes many people to complain. "Nice" hair has always been a sign of beauty, but nice has had many definitions over the centuries—powdered wigs were once the popular hairstyle.

Teenagers are notorious for being preoccupied with their hair—worrying about what the weather will be like on the night of a special date and how their hair will respond. They are known to spend hours trying to coax their naturally stick-straight or corkscrew-curly hair into the opposite texture or "stretch" their shorn locks after a haircut that didn't come out the way they pictured it. This is understandable because we live in a society that places so much emphasis on looks.

One of the bonuses about getting older is that you generally come to accept your hair. In fact, very often people who as teens hated their type of hair grow up to not only accept but appreciate their hair for the way it is. In most cases, nature doesn't make a mistake—the color and texture of the hair you were born with is usually what goes best with your face and skin coloring.

Whether you like or hate your hair, keeping it clean and in good condition goes a long way toward making you look and feel more attractive. Here are some simple tips for making the most of the hair you've got:

○ **Shampooing.** Depending upon whether your hair and scalp are oily, normal, or dry, you may need to shampoo every day, every other day, or once a week. Tepid—not too hot, not too cold—water is best for all hair types, and mild shampoos are usually a good bet. In fact, as you experiment with different hair products, you'll probably find that the more complicated the formula sounds and the more expensive it is, the less good it will do your hair. Simple, cheap shampoos that promise only to wash away dirt and oil generally do the best job.

Use your fingertips, not your nails, to gently scrub your scalp. If you wash your hair every day, one shampoo is plenty. Be sure to rinse

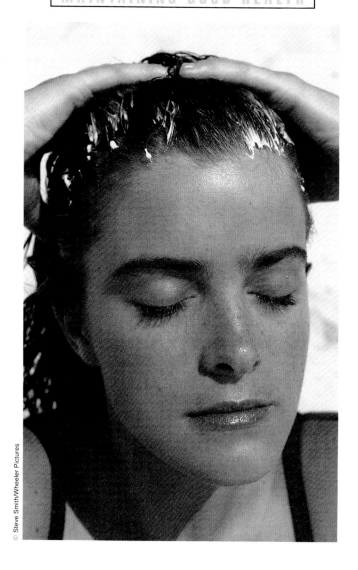

© Steve Smith/Wheeler Pictures

your hair thoroughly in order to get all of the soap out and maximize the shine.

○ **Conditioning.** The idea of *needing* a conditioner after shampooing is an invention of the modern cosmetic industry. If your hair seems dried out and dull looking, probably what it really needs is less abuse. Use a milder shampoo, and wash your hair less frequently. Give your hair a break from blow dryers and curling irons, and reconsider getting another perm or coloring your hair. Being kinder to your hair will get it into better condition, naturally.

However, if you like the smooth texture a conditioner gives your hair, use one. Again, the cheaper, simpler varieties are often best. Keep in mind that *all* a conditioner really does is coat each shaft of hair to make it lie flatter and feel silkier and softer.

○ **Drying.** The invention of home blow dryers led to the need for products that would counteract their harmful drying effects. Give your hair a break from blow drying once in a while, and let it dry naturally. If you don't like the way your hair looks when it air dries, then let it dry naturally most of the way and finish up with a blow dryer for a minute or two. Many of us complain that our hair "has a mind of its own." If this is true for you, it's better to go with your hair's natural tendencies instead of fighting them. There are plenty of hairstyles. Choose one that suits your hair instead of forcing your hair to suit a style.

Getting the Most from Hair-Styling Products

- *Gel*—works best when used sparingly (a nickel-size dollop is plenty) and on hair that is air-dried—both using too much gel and blow drying can cause flaking.

- *Mousse*—works best on fine or thin hair and when used in conjunction with blow drying. Rub a marshmallow-size dollop between hands, and run fingers through hair. Many styling mousses contain chemicals that dry out hair when used too often—try to use it no more than every other day.

- *Pomade and Oil*—work best on Black hair, which needs more moisturizing in order to style than Caucasian hair. Also works well on any type of coarse, kinky hair.

- *Hair Spray*—works on any type of hair to "set" style in place. Use sparingly, and spray at least six inches away from hair for best results.

Lice don't discriminate—anyone can catch them. And catching them from someone who is infested is the only way to get them; you don't get them from not being able to wash your hair for two days because you're sick. If you think you have lice, see your doctor immediately (before you infect anyone else). He or she will give you medicated shampoos and soaps that will get rid of the problem.

Scalping Stories

We generally don't give our scalp much thought unless there's something wrong with it. The most common scalp problem is dandruff. Called *seborrhea dermatitis,* dandruff is characterized by fine, white flaky scales of skin that drift like snow (but are not nearly as pretty) off your scalp and onto your shoulders. For those who have it, dandruff can be embarrassing and annoying, but it is nothing to worry about. It's a condition that, although usually persistant, can be controlled by any of the dandruff shampoos on the market.

Another common scalp problem is *lice.* Lice are small insects that live in hair by sucking blood from underneath the skin. Lice are not particular about the scalps they choose to live in. Which means you are not immune to catching it simply because you live in a clean home in a middle-class community. An itchy scalp is the first sign that you've been exposed to lice, and if you examine your hair you may find "nits," which are the eggs that lice hatch. Lice look like tiny gray dots and are harder to see than nits, which are white and attach tightly to hair shafts. You should contact your doctor as soon as you suspect you have lice. He or she will recommend medicated shampoos, creams, lotions, or soaps that kill lice. Your doctor will also tell you how to prevent reinfestation and spreading (washing all clothing and bedding in very hot water, etc.).

Lice also sometimes plant themselves in the pubic area. This type of infestation is called *crab lice,* or just *crabs,* because this form of the insect looks like a miniature crab. Unlike head lice, pubic lice is nearly always transmitted from one person to another by sexual contact. It's treated in the same manner as head lice.

Anatomy of a Pimple

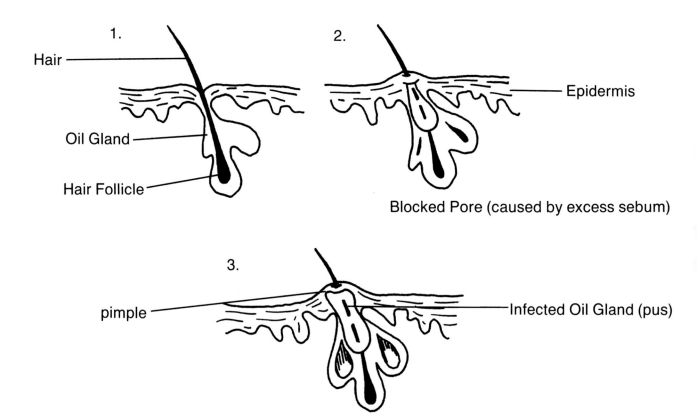

1.

Hair

Oil Gland

Hair Follicle

2.

Epidermis

Blocked Pore (caused by excess sebum)

3.

pimple

Infected Oil Gland (pus)

Skin Sins

The teen years are notorious for being a time of life when many people suffer from skin problems. Increased hormonal activity that causes your body to mature and become capable of reproduction is often responsible for changes in your skin (see Human Sexuality). If you're like most teenagers, your skin is oilier now than it ever has been, and you probably never know whether you'll be greeted in the morning by a brand new pimple on your face.

Acne is produced when excess oil and bacteria become trapped beneath plugs in the surface of your skin. As you may know too well, the results are red, bumpy irritations and eruptions on your skin. Dermatologists (skin doctors) used to think that certain foods caused acne. Potato chips, chocolate, french fries, and greasy burgers were thought to be common culprits. The current thinking is that these foods cause skin problems only if you are allergic to them or if you consume them in great quantities. (See Nutrition.)

A natural increase in oil produced by your sebaceous glands plus stress (see "Stress and Skin", page 36) are now thought to be the most common reasons for adolescent skin problems. If your acne is severe—if you have many pimples at any one time—you may need to see a dermatolo-

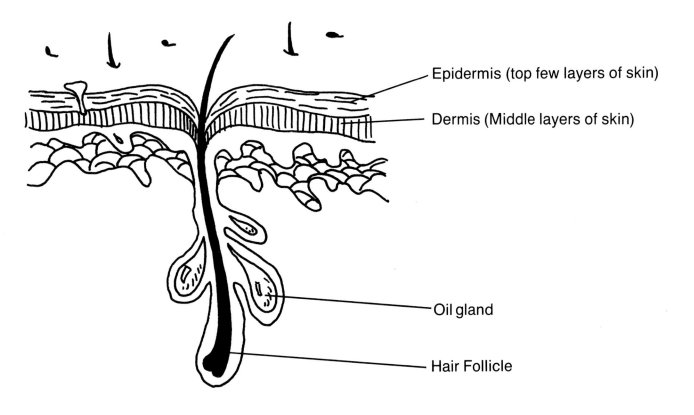

Epidermis (top few layers of skin)

Dermis (Middle layers of skin)

Oil gland

Hair Follicle

gist to improve your condition. In the meantime, try to remind yourself often that you are *still* a good person with many attractive qualities. Don't equate your sense of self-worth with how clear your skin is. The more self-conscious you are about your skin, the more everyone around you will be aware of it. And chances are the more you'll be touching and picking at your skin, which will only worsen the problem.

There will always be cruel individuals who get pleasure out of tormenting people about their looks, but for the most part, you'll find that people will respond to the signals you give out. If your attitude says, "I think I'm a gross-looking person because of the pimples on my face," others will perceive you that way. Nobody who has ever lived through teenage acne will tell you it was easy. But as with everything else in life, it's up to you to make the best or the worst of it.

There are some things you can do to help improve your complexion. In fact, you don't even have to buy a lot of expensive skin-care products to do it—many of the best skin-care products are found in your refrigerator, cupboard, and medicine cabinet. For centuries milk, avocado, egg whites, and other foods have been used to help soothe and smooth skin. Here are a few natural (and cheap) skin-smoothers to try:

Steaming

Chamomile tea or *lemon slices* (for all skin types). Put a towel tent over your head, and steam your face about twelve inches (thirty centimeters) over a pot of hot water with a handful of chamomile tea flowers or lemon slices in it for a nice fragrance. The steam will open your pores so you can clean them. Steam for about ten minutes, then wash your face as you normally do.

Scrubs

Crushed almonds and honey (for normal to dry skin). Mix crushed almonds with just enough honey to make a paste. The honey traps moisture in your skin, and the nuts remove dirt and oil from your pores. Gently rub the mixture into your skin with your fingers, massaging in small circles. Rinse with tepid water.

Crushed almonds and water (for oily to normal skin). This is the same as the mixture above, except substitute a drop of water for the honey because you don't need to moisturize.

A clean washcloth (for all skin types). A washcloth is better for sloughing away dead skin than commercial scrub pads, which are often harsh and difficult to get clean after use.

Masks

Egg whites (for oily skin). Spread egg whites over your face, and then rinse with cool water when they start to stiffen. This is a great pore tightener.
Avocado (for normal to dry skin). Peel a ripe avocado, leaving a little of the fruit on the inside of the peel. Rub the inside of the peel against your face. The gritty texture of the peel scrubs skin gently while the avocado fruit moisturizes. Leave the residue on for a few minutes, and rinse with cool water. (Mix some finely chopped garlic and a little lemon juice with the leftover mashed avocado, and you have guacomole. Eat it with tortilla chips.)

Store-bought facial masks are often expensive and are unnecessary if you know how to make your own natural (and cheap!) masks.

Toners

Witch hazel (for oily to normal skin). Witch hazel is an effective, mild astringent. It tightens pores as rubbing alcohol or alcohol-based astringents do, but without the over-drying that comes with alcohol. Dry patches on top of pimples present a double problem of dealing with dry and oily skin at the same time.

Milk (for normal to dry skin). Cool milk dabbed on with a cotton pad and rinsed off a minute or two later is a great skin soother. It calms down red, inflamed (sore) skin, sensitive skin, and dry, flaky, windburned skin.

Commercial Skin-Care Best Bets

Mild cleansers. These are best. Even for blemished skin, a mild facial cleansing bar is most effective.

Benzoyl peroxide drying agents. These work well for acne but should be used sparingly and cautiously on minor breakouts.

Simple moisturizers. The ones without added fragrances are best. Use them only where skin is dry. If a moisturizer seems too rich for your skin— if it sits on your face looking greasy and doesn't sink in—dilute it with a drop or two of water in the palm of your hand.

© Steve Smith/Wheeler Pictures

Be sure to use moisturizer on only those parts of our face and body that look and feel dry, tight, or flaky. Over-moisturizing can lead to breakouts.

he Fine Art of Shaving

Learning how to shave your beard, legs, or underarms can be a frustrating and sometimes painful experience. Here are a few pointers to help you get through it smoothly.

○ The best time to shave your beard is immediately after you shower. Don't even open your bathroom door all the way—the steamy atmosphere keeps your skin soft and your facial hairs standing up. This makes them easier to shave off. (For more information, see Human Sexuality)

○ The best time to shave your underarms and legs is while you're in the shower. If this seems like tricky acrobatics, shave right after your shower.

○ Make sure your skin is as clean and as oil-free as possible before you begin shaving. Dirt and oil flatten hair shafts, and you don't get a close shave.

○ Soap and shaving cream usually work best as lubricants for shaving your face, legs, or underarms. It's a good idea to let the lather sit on your skin for a couple of minutes before you start shaving. This gives the soap or cream time to soften coarse hairs.

○ Shaving strokes—with the grain, against the grain—are a matter of practice and personal preference. The best advice is to experiment and find out which method works best for you.

○ When you have outbreaks of acne, it's best not to shave your face or to shave as infrequently as possible until pimples go away. Dragging a razor across your blemished face will only aggravate your skin problems.

○ Keep your razor clean, change disposable razors frequently, and run your razor under hot water before, during, and after your shave.

○ If you're cutting yourself regularly, it may be because your razor is too old or dirty, you're pressing down on your skin too hard, or you're holding the razor incorrectly (the blade should always be at a horizontal angle from your skin). A styptic pencil or a bit of tissue applied with a little pressure is usually all that is needed to stop the bleeding.

© Overseas Constellaz/Envision

A Word on Picking at Your Skin

Don't do it. It only prolongs the process of healing and can leave permanent scars on your face even after the pimples have subsided. Don't use abrasive cloths or scrubs on inflamed pimples. The best way to get rid of blackheads—thick oil plugs in your skin that turn black when in contact with air on the surface of your skin—is to steam your face and then follow with a scrub. If this doesn't do it, and you insist on removing your blackheads manually, wash your hands, wrap tissues around each index finger, and as quickly and gently as possible, squeeze the area surrounding the blackhead to force the clog out. Rinse your face with warm water when you're done. If your face is red and blotchy afterward, you will know you were too rough.

Stress and Skin

If stress can cause a heart attack, then it's easy to believe that stress can make pimples pop out on your face. Hives, cold sores, and other skin irritations can also be brought on by stress. Pimples that suddenly appear on your face the week your mother is getting remarried are most likely not coincidental. Stressful times don't have to be unhappy times—you may be happy that your mother is remarrying, but it is a time of adjustment, and you are feeling the strain. Skin problems caused by stress are like little voices offstage cuing us to calm down, to take things easier. The problem is that looking in a mirror at a face with a cold sore or four new zits can cause *more* stress. Try not to let it. Take it for the cue it is, and relax. This, too, will pass. (For further information on stress, see Stress and Mental Health.)

SPF

SUN PROTECTION FACTOR	FOR YOUR SKIN TYPE
2–4	Burn rarely, tan easily
5–6	Minimal burning, tan well
7–9	Burn moderately, tan gradually
9–14	Burn easily, tan minimally
15 and over	Burn easily, never tan

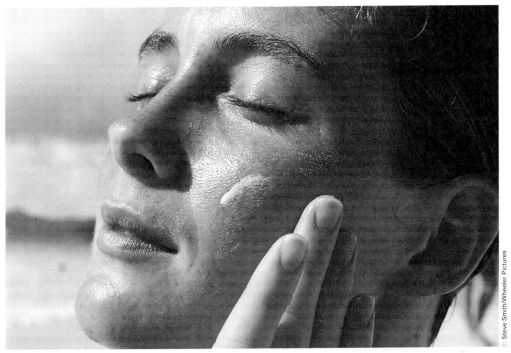

© Steve Smith/Wheeler Pictures

Old Man Sol: The Price of a Suntan

It is one of life's cruel ironies that a suntan looks so good, because it is so bad for you. There's no doubt that repeated prolonged exposure to the sun's ultraviolet rays at best will make you more wrinkled as you age and at worst will put you at high risk of developing skin cancer. You're at even higher risk if you're fair-skinned, but dark-skinned sun worshippers also are at risk. One more rotten irony is that fair-skinned people are often the ones who most desire a tan. You may fall into the lucky percentage of suntanners who don't get skin cancer, but even if you do, you probably won't be able to escape the short-term painful sunburns and long-term premature aging and wrinkling effects.

Dermatologists sometimes advise fair-skinned people who burn easily to avoid the sun as much as possible. But if you live in a warm climate or take part in outdoor activities, this advice is difficult to follow. Besides, taken in small doses, the sun is good for you. It provides your body with vitamin D and gives your mind and spirits a boost.

You need, however, to be wise about your sun exposure. Avoid being in the sun for extended periods of time between eleven A.M. and three P.M., when the sun's burning rays are strongest. *Always* wear a sunscreen that's strong enough for your skin type (see chart above).

Most sunscreen and tanning products come with a number labelled SPF, or *sun protection factor*. Take the SPF number and multiply it by the number of minutes you can usually be in the sun without burning and you'll get the new total number of minutes you can be in the sun if you are protected by this sunscreen. For instance, if you're fair-skinned and can only stand the sun for about twenty minutes before you start burning, choose a sunscreen with an SPF of four. With this protection, you'll be safe in the sun for eighty minutes before you begin to burn. If you're planning on playing basketball outdoors or swimming at the beach, an hour and twenty minutes of protection is not going to be enough. You should use a sunscreen with maximum protection, an SPF of fifteen or higher, to avoid getting burned.

After you've chosen a sunscreen, you should be sure to use it properly. To allow it time to sink in and work best, a sunscreen should be applied about thirty minutes before going outside. Be sure you apply it evenly. The spots you miss will get more sun, and your skin will end up a splotchy, blotchy mess.

Sunscreens, *even if they say they're waterproof,* need to be reapplied frequently, especially when you've been swimming or sweating. Protect sensitive areas—nose, backs of knees, lips—with a stronger sunblock like zinc oxide cream.

If you're taking any medication you may be at increased risk of sunburn. Tetracycline, birth control pills, sulfa drugs, antihistamines, diuretics, and antidepressants increase the user's sensitivity to the sun. It's also best not to wear perfumes or cosmetics as they often cause the same reactions.

You *can* enjoy the sun without paying too dear a price. But remember that even if you conscientiously use a sunscreen, if you habitually sunbathe for hours at a time, your skin will show the signs of premature aging sooner than you think. Sunscreens keep you from burning; they don't prevent your skin from tanning. Even perfect tans fade. Is the temporary pleasure worth the permanent scars?

© Susanna Pashko/Envision

For many years, people invented all kinds of methods to achieve a suntan, including foil sheets that reflect the sun back onto the face or body. Today people are more aware of the long term dangers of a suntan (skin cancer, wrinkles, etc.), and they are beginning to recognize that a tan is not as attractive as it once was.

Sunburn Antidotes

- cool baths or showers
- aspirin
- drinking plenty of water and juices
- cool compresses
- a warm blanket
- gel from a fresh aloe plant
- see a doctor if your sunburn causes nausea, fever, severe blistering or intense pain

© Kozlowski/ FPG International

The Bare Bones Basics of First Aid

Here and throughout this book, mini first-aid sections offer quick-study help for health emergencies. These are not a substitute for a first-aid course (check with your local Red Cross or community center for details). To locate a first-aid section in this book, turn to the section dealing with the part of the body in need of aid. For example, first-aid for poisoning is in "The Digestive System and Intestines" section.

Burns

Type of Burns	*Symptoms*	*What To Do*
First degree (minor)	Damage limited to epidermis, outer layer of skin; redness, some swelling. (Most sunburns are first-degree burns.)	Apply ice or cold water compresses for about a half hour. If no blisters, apply petroleum jelly and gauze dressing. For sunburn treatments, see "Sunburn Antidotes," page 39.
Second degree (major)	Damage extends through epidermis to dermis, next layer of skin; blistering.	If burn doesn't cover large area, gently clean with soap and water and rinse with a saline (saltwater) solution; get medical help if burn is extensive.
Third degree (severe)	Damage extends through full thickness of skin; complete destruction of skin and sometimes underlying tissue.	Call for medical help immediately; immerse burned area in ice water; wrap loosely in clean sheet or cloth; *do not* try to remove clothing that's adhered to burn or apply any ointment; lie victim down with feet elevated, and keep him or her still.
Chemical burn	Damage to skin or eyes caused by contact with corrosive chemical.	Flush area with lots of cold, running water, being careful not to wash chemical onto other parts of the body; follow first-aid instruction on product if given; cover burn with a cold, wet, sterile dressing.
Electrical burn	Caused by direct contact with electrical current.	Don't touch victim while he or she is in contact with electric current; shut off source of current or remove victim from it with a dry stick or rope; check victim's breathing; if necessary, start cardiopulmonary resuscitation (CPR—see page 64); begin first aid and/or call for medical help.

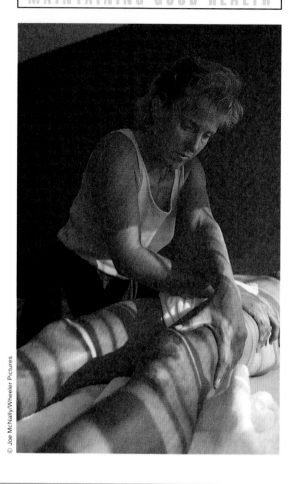

© Joe McNally/Wheeler Pictures

he Bare Bones Basics of First Aid

Deep or Large Skin Wounds

1. Lie down and elevate injured part, if possible. Call for medical help.

2. Pick out any visible and easily removed debris from wound—don't try to remove deeply embedded debris.

3. With a clean cloth, handkerchief, or your fingers, press hard on wound to stop bleeding. Hold edges of wound together if they're gaping, and keep pressing down. Direct pressure *around* instead of on top of anything imbedded in wound.

4. When bleeding stops, call for medical help if necessary, and apply a clean pad or cloth and tie it around wound. Add more padding as needed; don't remove previous pad.

Your Eyes, Ears, and Nose

Out of Sight

Very few people are fortunate enough to go through life without ever having a vision problem. If you escape needing glasses when you're young, chances are you'll need them sometime later in life. Heredity and occupation determine whether or not you'll have vision problems and at what time in your life you will have them.

Myopia, being able to see things clearly close up, but not at a distance, and *hyperopia*, being able to see things better at a distance, but seeing both near and far objects blurred, are the two most common vision problems. (One in every six people is myopic.) Luckily, both problems can be corrected with glasses or contact lenses.

You'll know you probably need glasses if your eyes feel sore and strained a lot of the time, and when you gradually begin to realize that things seem to have lost their sharpness. Everything around you begins to resemble an Impressionist painting—blurry images that get clearer if you squint your eyes. Don't put off seeing an eye doctor once you suspect you have a vision problem. The problem will not go away, it will only get worse. Besides, today there are so many choices of good-looking eyeglass frames and comfortable contact lenses that even the vainest of us has no excuse for not getting his or her eyes checked. If you're myopic, keep in mind that your vision may worsen during your teenage years, but then it generally improves as you get older.

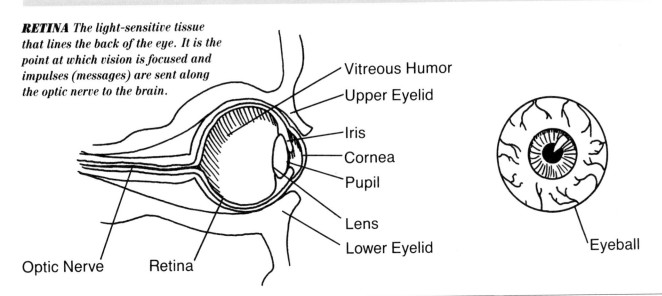

RETINA *The light-sensitive tissue that lines the back of the eye. It is the point at which vision is focused and impulses (messages) are sent along the optic nerve to the brain.*

Vitreous Humor
Upper Eyelid
Iris
Cornea
Pupil
Lens
Lower Eyelid
Optic Nerve
Retina
Eyeball

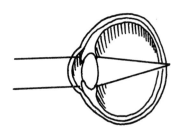

Farsighted *(Hypertropic)*
Eyeball is too short, and light comes to a focal point beyond the retina

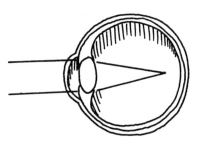

Nearsighted *(Myopic)*
Eyeball is too long, and light reaches a focal point just short of the retina

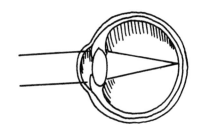

Normal Eye

Caring for Contacts

If you have a vision problem, there's a good chance you're one of more than twenty-three million Americans who wear contact lenses. When contacts first arrived on the market, there wasn't much choice. It was hard lenses or nothing. Today you have a choice of hard or soft, daily- or extended-wear, and clear or tinted lenses that can even make your brown eyes blue.

Contacts do, however, come with a hitch: You've got to care for them much more carefully than you do eyeglasses. After all, lenses are put *in* your eyes, not in front of them, and anything you put in contact with your body carries risks.

Studies have disclosed several types of bacterial infections, especially with regard to extended-wear lenses. Some doctors are concerned particularly about an infection of the cornea (the translucent covering over the center of your eye) called *Acanthamoeba keratitis*. This infection occurs most often among people who wear soft contact lenses on a daily basis. The infection is the result of an amoeba that causes the cornea to swell and break down—some people have even had to have corneal transplants. The infection is very painful and treatment is difficult and time-consuming.

Some opthalmologists (eye doctors with an M.D.) think extended-wear lenses are more dangerous because of the length of time they stay in your eyes—up to two weeks. Others believe daily-wear lenses are more dangerous because daily handling and improper care can cause infections. Regardless of who is right, it's clear that caring for your contacts conscientiously goes a long way toward preventing infection. Below are tips on how to care for soft lenses:

○ Always wash and rinse your hands thoroughly before handling lenses. It's a good idea not to dry your hands with a towel before you handle your lenses, just rinse and leave them wet. Otherwise, fibers from the towel will stick to your lenses.

○ Use commercially prepared, nonpreserved saline solution.

○ Disinfect your lenses with *either* a commercial chemical solution or thermally, with a heating unit. Once you've chosen a method, you *must* stick with it.

○ Never put your lens in your mouth to wet it and then put it in your eye; the germs in your mouth are not meant to be in your eye.

○ Don't use tap or distilled water to clean your lenses—the water may be contaminated.

○ Don't wear your lenses while swimming—you may lose them or get an infection from the bacteria or chemicals in the water.

○ Follow the manufacturer's directions for caring for your type of contact lenses.

A Word About Sharing Eye Makeup

DON'T DO IT. It's one of the most common ways eye infections are passed. Using old cosmetics is also a bad idea. Be sure to replace mascara every three months.

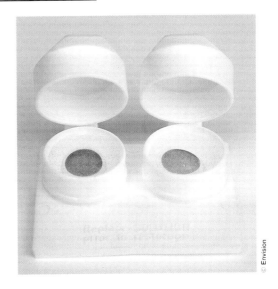

Five Tips for Preventing Eye Infections

1. Use only your own washcloths and towels.

2. Do not touch the area around your eyes with dirty hands.

3. Insert, remove, and clean contact lenses as directed.

4. Wet contacts with the proper solution, not saliva or tap water.

5. Stop using eye cosmetics that cause irritation or redness. Make sure applicators for eye cosmetics are clean. Buy new mascara every three months.

© Grace Davies/Envision

The Knowing Nose

You may not love the way your nose looks these days—the nose tends to "mature" earlier than the rest of the face. The great majority of the time, however, the rest of the face catches up eventually, and all your features suddenly work together.

Even if you think your nose is kind of funny-looking right now, one thing you can't accuse your nose of is stupidity. The olfactory nerve that is triggered when you smell something is like a storage room of memories. Novelists have written flowery passages about the power of scent to conjure up thoughts of people and places in the past. One whiff of crayons can instantly transport

you to kindergarten. The scent of a just-mown lawn can trigger memories of summers past. A trail of a familiar perfume left in the air as someone passes can make you turn to see if the wearer is the person with whom you identify the scent. And it wouldn't be Thanksgiving if the whole house didn't smell like roasted turkey.

In fact, eating would be simply a way to stay alive if it weren't for our sense of smell. When you have a cold and can't smell anything, you don't have much of an appetite, right? Our taste-buds are severely affected when our sense of smell goes on strike. So even if your nose isn't as perfect looking as you'd like, give it a little respect—it's a finely tuned source of pleasure and a treasure chest of memories.

he Bare Bones Basics of First Aid

Nosebleeds

Nosebleeds are common and usually minor emergencies that result from facial injuries, nose infections, or high blood pressure. Here's how to treat them:

○ Sit up so that blood trickling down your throat doesn't get into your lungs.

○ Apply pressure to stop the bleeding by pinching your nostrils or by placing a clean wad of cloth or tissue between your upper gums and the underside of your upper lip and then pressing on it.

○ Keep calm and quiet—anxiety can raise your blood pressure and increase bleeding.

○ Hold an icepack on your nose.

○ If your nose still doesn't stop bleeding, get medical help.

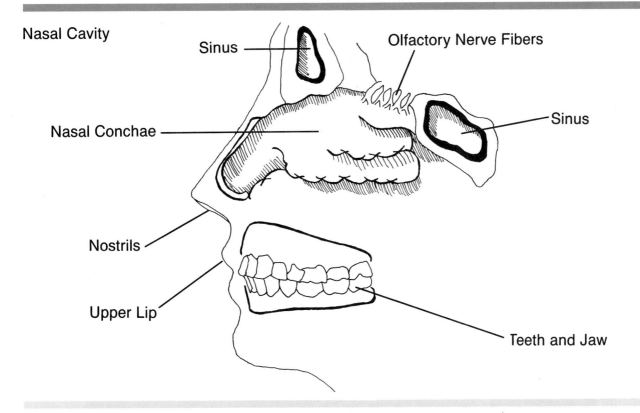

Nasal Cavity

Sinus

Olfactory Nerve Fibers

Sinus

Nasal Conchae

Nostrils

Upper Lip

Teeth and Jaw

What's That Ringing in My Ear?

A walk down a busy urban street. A night of babysitting a cranky four-month-old. Seeing a heavy metal band in concert. What these diverse activities have in common is that they are all assaults on your sense of hearing. Sirens, jack-hammers, car horns, a baby's screams, and loud music can have annoying short-term and serious long-term effects on your hearing. Loud noise is defined as noise twenty decibels (a unit used to define degrees of loudness) above normal conversation. A baby's screams can be thirty decibels above normal conversation, and some rock concerts can be a lot louder.

The immediate effect this level of noise has on your ears is a ringing, buzzing, or hissing that can last a day or two after the noise is gone. These sounds are a condition called tinnitus, and it can be extremely annoying. Continued exposure to loud noise will eventually do permanent damage to your hearing.

Experts also think tinnitus can be triggered by other things. A head injury, a migraine, an ear infection, allergies, impacted ear wax, high blood pressure, use of some drugs (affecting hearing and balance) like aspirin and antibiotics, tobacco and marijuana, and birth control pills can all cause your ears to ring.

Once you have tinnitus, you pretty much have to just wait it out. The best treatment is prevention. Here's how:

○ Avoid repeated exposure to loud noise. If you must be around loud noises frequently, protect your ears with external earmuffs, soft wax, or foam earplugs that conform to the shape of your ear canal.
○ Avoid daily use of aspirin.
○ It's best not to use headphones, but if you do, keep the volume down.
○ Don't use cotton-tipped swabs to try to remove ear wax. Ear wax generally does not need to be removed, and poking around deep in your ear canal could harm you.

Noise Levels in Our Environment

Sound	Noise Level in Decibels	Human Response
	0	Threshold of Hearing
	10	Just Audible
Broadcasting Studio	20	
Soft Whisper (15 feet)		
Library	30	Very Quiet
Bedroom		
Living Room	40	
Light Auto Traffic (100 feet)	50	Quiet
Air Conditioning Unit (20 feet)	60	Intrusive
Freeway Traffic (50 feet)	70	Telephone Use Difficult
Freight Train (50 feet)		
Alarm Clock	80	Annoying
Pneumatic Drill (50 feet)		
Heavy Truck (50 feet)	90	Hearing Damage
N.Y.C. Subway Station		(after 8 hours)
Garbage Truck	100	Very Annoying
Jet Takeoff (2,000 feet)		
Riveting Machine		
	110	
		Maximum Vocal Effort
Auto Horn (3 feet)	120	
Amplified Rock Music		
Jet Takeoff (200 feet)	130	
Jet Operation	140	
Carrier Deck		Painfully Loud
	150	

The Ins and Outs of the Ear

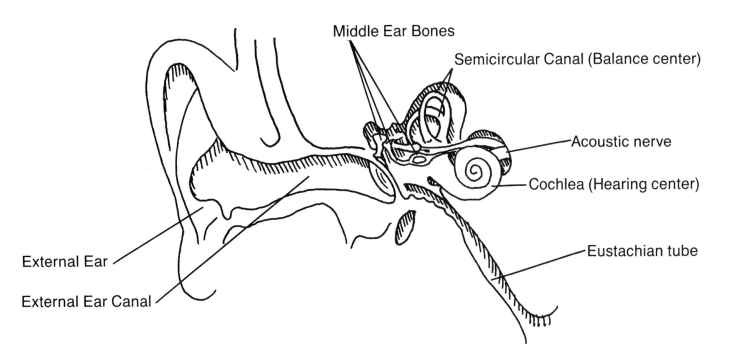

Middle Ear Bones

Semicircular Canal (Balance center)

Acoustic nerve

Cochlea (Hearing center)

Eustachian tube

External Ear

External Ear Canal

Parts of a Tooth

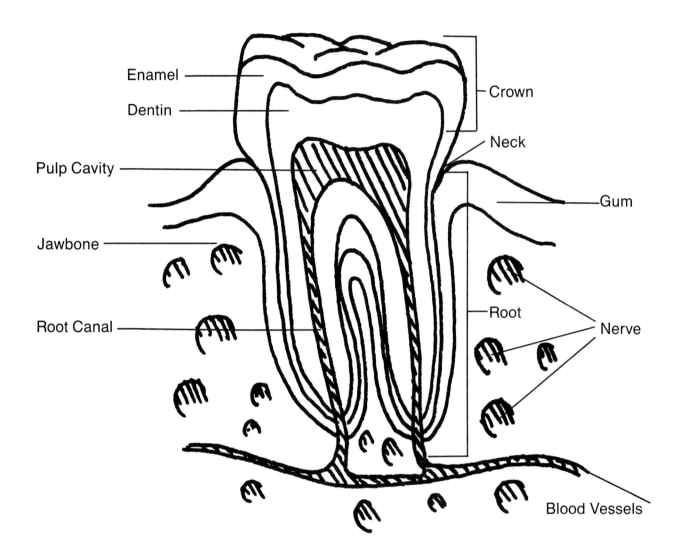

Enamel

Dentin

Pulp Cavity

Jawbone

Root Canal

Crown

Neck

Gum

Root

Nerve

Blood Vessels

Your Mouth, Gums, and Teeth

Good dental habits don't come easily. It takes discipline to brush your teeth at least twice a day and floss at least once a day. But like all habits, you only have to force yourself to do these tasks for a short while—maybe a few weeks. After that, the tasks become habit. After the habit takes over, if you *don't* brush and floss your teeth, you feel weird. But before you can make brushing and flossing a habit, you have to know the right way to do it.

Brushing

First of all, what kind of a toothbrush should you use? Most dentists recommend a brush with soft bristles because they're gentler on gums. Choose a head size that makes it easy for you to reach all parts of your mouth—some dentists advise adults to use child's size toothbrushes for this reason. Keep your brush clean, don't lend it to anyone, and replace it every few months. For the best brushing results and less wear and tear on your gum line, dentists recommend placing your toothbrush at a forty-five-degree angle on your gums and brushing up from your lower teeth and down from your upper teeth. Be sure to brush in the same direction on all outer and inner surfaces of your teeth. On the chewing surfaces and behind your teeth, use a back-and-forth motion. When you feel like you're ready to stop brushing, brush a few seconds more.

Flossing

Flossing is important for removing trapped food and *plaque*, which is a soft, sticky bacteria that builds up on teeth and can cause gum disease. If not removed for a couple of days, such as when you don't floss and brush, plaque will harden into a cement-like substance called tartar. It may be a little trickier to get the hang of flossing, but with practice you will. Holding the floss taut between your thumb and forefinger (with about one inch between the fingers), guide it gently down between teeth. Try not to snap it too quickly down onto gums. Curve the floss into a C shape around the sides of each tooth. Then use an up-and-down motion—not a sawing motion—to get at plaque between teeth and just below your gum line. Advance to clean floss as you work around your mouth by winding the used portion around your fingers.

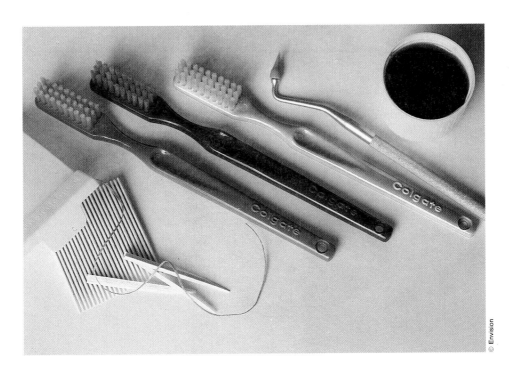

© Envision

Avoiding Cavities

About ninety-five out of every 100 Americans have some tooth decay. You may not be able to avoid getting cavities, also called *dental caries,* but you can control how many you get. Using a fluoride toothpaste, brushing at least twice a day, flossing once a day, and limiting the number of sweets and sticky foods (such as raisins) you eat should help you keep tooth decay to a minimum. Visiting your dentist regularly for checkups and cleanings will also help you limit your less pleasant visits to him or her for fillings, drillings, and pulled teeth. (For more information on the basics of good dental care, see Nutrition.)

Do You Have Bad Breath?

Whew! Is it the garlic pizza you ate last night or is something wrong? You've got bad breath, and even if nobody points it out to you, you probably know it. If it's a persistent problem, bad breath, or *halitosis,* is usually the result of tooth decay and *periodontal* (gum) disease. Having a nose, tonsil, or sinus infection can cause your breath to smell bad too. And, of course, it could also be the garlic pizza, but that will subside after about a day and won't recur until the next time you eat another pungent food.

Masking the odor of bad breath doesn't help much—the freshening effect of mouthwashes and breath sprays are short-lived. It's better to try to get rid of the cause of the bad breath. Have your dental problems taken care of by your dentist. Avoid future dental problems by avoiding cavity-causing foods and taking care of your teeth and gums. See your doctor to help get rid of any tonsil or sinus infection you might have. And if you're a garlic, onion, or spicy-food lover, make sure your friends eat the same foods you eat—that way you won't notice or be able to complain about each other's breath.

How a Cavity Grows

A break in the enamel . . .

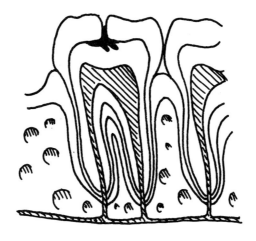

. . . allows decay to enter the tooth and spread, . . .

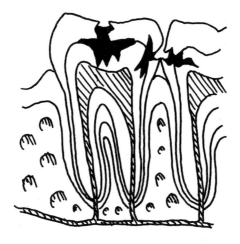

. . . leading to infection in the root if the cavity is untreated.

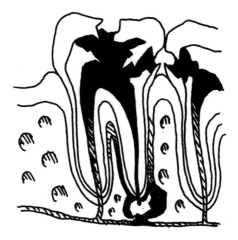

© Blumensaadt/Wheeler Pictures

Your Neck, Back, Arms, and Hands

Neck and Neck, Back to Back

Your neck or back may be your body's weak spot. Many people, especially adults who lead fast-paced lives and work in pressure-filled jobs, hold a lot of tension in their necks. Many more people have back problems. In fact, doctors estimate that four out of five Americans suffer from back pain at some point in their lives. For most of these people, the pain is in their lower back, also called the *lumbar region.* Eighty-five percent of the time this kind of pain is due to weakness in the muscles surrounding the spine.

What makes your back muscles weak? The main culprits are obesity, poor posture, and a sedentary lifestyle, all of which lead to poor general muscle tone. These problems are totally preventable. By exercising regularly, keeping your weight down, and using common sense when lifting heavy objects (*always* bend at the knees), you stand a good chance of avoiding back problems.

As for neck problems, the most effective way to reduce tension in your neck is to relax. Easier said than done? Maybe, but there *are* simple ways of relaxing this part of your body, such as stretching exercises, head rolls, meditation (see page 106), and yoga (see page 76).

Smart Back Exercises

The following exercises are good for *gently* strengthening your lower back and abdominal muscles. The problem with most back exercises is that your back needs to already be strong in order to withstand the stress of the exercises. The exercises below avoid this problem by not putting any undue stress on your back and by helping to build your abdominal muscles, which further support your back. (See also Exercise.) **Check with your doctor before you begin any exercise program, including this one.**

1. *The Pelvic Tilt.* Lie on your back with your arms at your sides, palms down, knees bent. Pull your stomach in so that the small of your back (the part that usually doesn't touch the floor when you're lying flat) touches the floor. Tighten your buttocks, lift your hips, and hold for ten seconds. Relax, and repeat twenty times.
2. *Bent-Leg Sit-Ups.* Lying in the same starting position as above, extend your arms out toward your knees and slowly raise your head, shoulders, and upper back to a thirty-degree angle above the floor. Hold for ten seconds, lie down, relax, and repeat twenty times.

    Note: You should *not* lift your whole back off the floor. This would put stress on your back. At first, simply try to lift your shoulder blades while keeping your lower back pressed into the floor. As your strength increases, try lifting your legs until they are perpendicular to the floor.

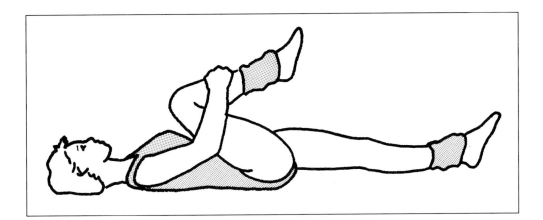

Lower Back Stretches: Lie on your back and bend your knees. Raise one leg, grasp the knee with both hands, and bring it to your chin. Hold for 10 counts, then release. Do the same with the other leg. Repeat the exercise 10 times for each leg.

Armed Forces

When Tony started Nautilus weight training, he thought that it would be a way of finally getting rid of his image as a no-muscle lightweight. Tony liked the results so much that he started going to the gym every night instead of three nights a week. A guy at the gym, a trainer, who was much more "built" than Tony, told him he could help him pump up faster. He gave Tony some pills and said that they'd "complement" his weight-training program. Tony figured if it worked for this guy, it would work for him, and getting bigger was all he cared about. Tony's mother discovered the pills in his room and took them to the pharmacy to have them analyzed. When she and his father sat him down for a talk that night, it was the first

Tony had heard about steroids and the dangers of them.

Anabolic steroids—synthetic male hormones—are anti-inflammatory drugs that have recently been abused by athletes, especially body builders. The drugs give builders a bulkier, more muscular look, which may pump up their confidence and give them an edge in competition but, at the same time, puts them at high risk of developing liver cancer. Other risks for men who use steroids include a decrease in the size of testes (where sperm is produced), impotence (inability to have an erection), and stunted growth. For women the risks include liver damage, increased facial hair, lowering of the voice, and menstrual irregularities. Basically, steroids are bad news. Do yourself and your body a favor, and don't use them. (See also *Substance Abuse.*)

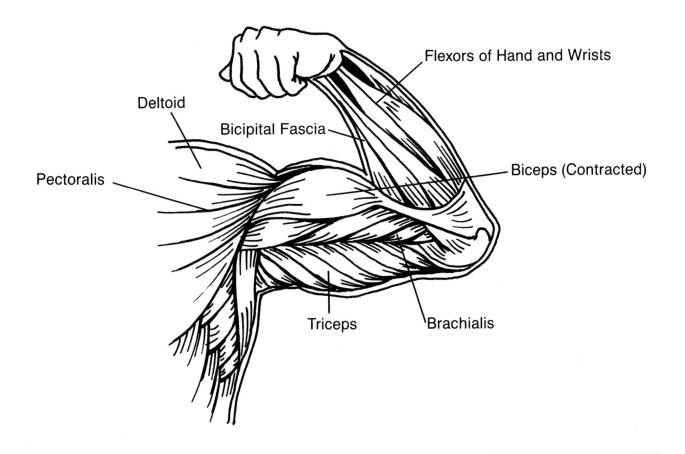

Flexors of Hand and Wrists

Deltoid

Bicipital Fascia

Biceps (Contracted)

Pectoralis

Triceps

Brachialis

Anti-perspirants and deodorants are products designed to alleviate some of the unpleasant effects of a perfectly natural process—underarm perspiration. Anti-perspirants contain chemicals that keep you from perspiring (nothing can stop perspiration competely, nor should it) and fragrances that make you smell better when you do perspire. Deodorants contain nothing to stop perspiration, only fragrances that mask perspiration odors. (See also *Human Sexuality.*)

Hand to Hand

There are people who think that the lines on your hand mean more than dry skin. These people are called palmists, or palm readers, and although many who practice on street corners today are likely to be more interested in the green paper in your palm than anything else, the practice of palm reading goes back to the days of ancient scholars like Aristotle, Pythagoras, and the poet Virgil. Here are what palmists say some of the lines on your hand represent. Take this information with several doses of your own common sense. You know yourself better than anyone knows you, and the way your life turns out is largely up to you.

○ *Life line.* The life line represents your life force from birth to death. A strong, clear line is thought to indicate a life with purpose and direction. A short or interrupted life line does *not* necessarily mean the owner will die an early or violent death; it may simply indicate an intense life. Keep in mind that palmists say our hand lines change as we grow and change.

○ *Head line.* The head line does not indicate how smart or stupid you are based on how long or short your line is. What it may indicate is your tendencies. A head line that begins high up toward your index finger may mean you tend to be self-reliant. If your head and life lines touch as they travel down your hand, it may mean that you sometimes lack self-confidence and doubt your abilities. A forked ending to the head line is called the "writer's fork," and its owner is often able to achieve commercial success through creative talent.

○ *Heart line.* A long, gradual curving line that begins under the index finger is thought to indicate a "feminine," romantic, and vulnerable personality. When this line begins between your index and middle fingers, it is thought to indicate a "masculine," sensual, and direct personality.

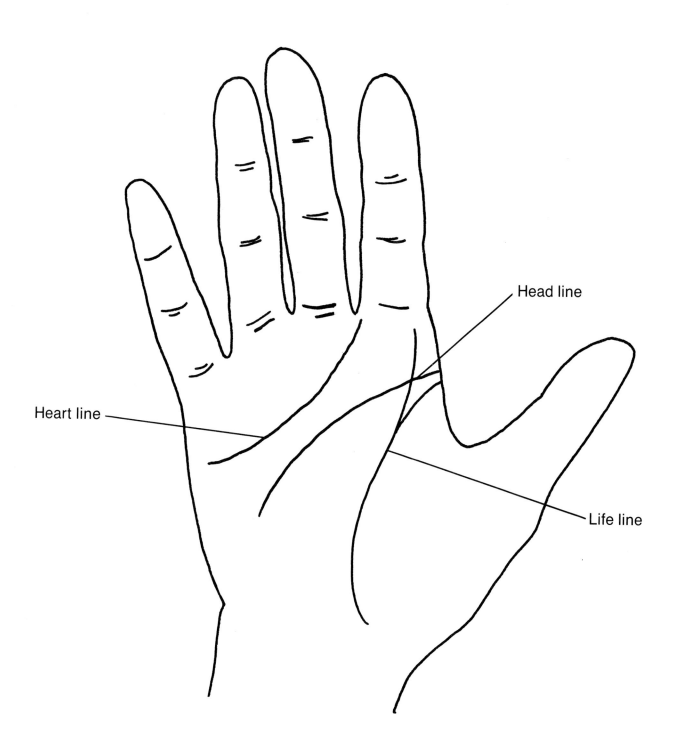

Head line

Heart line

Life line

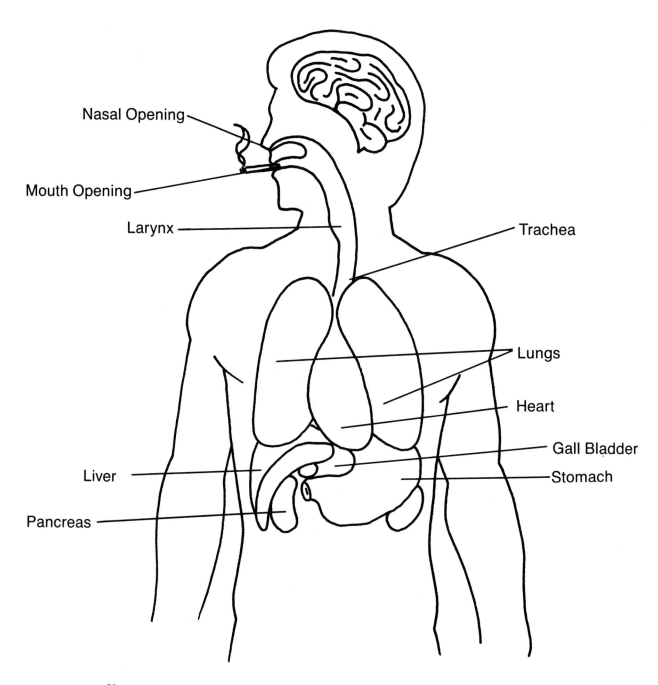

Nasal Opening

Mouth Opening

Larynx

Trachea

Lungs

Heart

Gall Bladder

Stomach

Liver

Pancreas

If you are a smoker, you are ten times more likely than a nonsmoker to die of lung cancer. But that's not all—you're also many times more likely to die of cancer of the mouth, throat, larynx, esophagus, stomach, pancreas, kidney, or bladder. And you're at much greater risk of suffering a heart attack. To smoke or not to smoke—the choice is up to you.

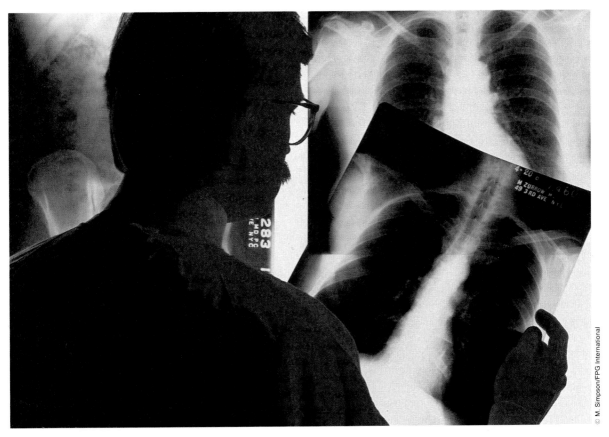

An X-ray is a photograph of you from the inside out. It enables your doctor to detect problems in your body that he would otherwise be unable to see. But having many X-rays taken is known to be dangerous. Don't be afraid to question your doctor if he recommends you have several X-rays.

© M. Simpson/FPG International

Your Chest, Lungs, and Heart

Take a Deep Breath

The dangers of cigarette smoking are well known (see Substance Abuse). But how do you actually benefit by *not* smoking, aside from probably living a longer life? Here are some of the immediate benefits of being—and staying—a nonsmoker.

10 Benefits to Not Smoking

1. Steadier, stronger heart

2. Healthier appetite

3. Wider blood vessels for blood to flow through freely

4. Lower blood pressure

5. Brain free of addiction to nicotine

6. Better working kidneys (which produce the urine to be flushed out of your body)

7. Sharper taste buds

8. Better breath

9. More money—you'll be a couple of dollars richer per day than a heavy smoker

10. Nonsmokers are more pleasant to be around.

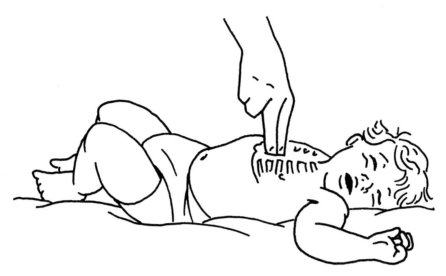

To perform CPR on a baby, place two fingers (rather than the heel of your hand for an older child or adult) on his chest along the center of his breastbone and push down one-half to one inch (1.25 to 2.5 centimeters) about 100 times a minute.

The Bare Bones Basics of First Aid

Cardiopulmonary Resuscitation (CPR)

When someone stops breathing, has no pulse, and begins to turn a bluish color, he or she needs *cardio* (heart) *pulmonary* (lungs) *resuscitation* (reviving) immediately. After only four or five minutes without oxygen, a person can suffer permanent brain damage, and seven or eight minutes without oxygen will cause death. Check with your local Red Cross for training in CPR. By learning this technique, you could save the life of someone you love. Remember, if at all possible, have someone else call for medical help *while* you are performing CPR—once you begin, you will not be able to stop until the victim regains consciousness.

Latest Developments

It's natural to compare your developing body with those of your friends. Deana's breasts are growing faster than Caroline's breasts. Michael has more hair on his chest than Blake does on his. But while you're checking out breast size and hairiness, keep in mind that there is no norm—everyone develops at their own pace, and yours might be faster or slower than your friends'. If by age fifteen you don't have much of a bust, it doesn't mean you never will. Many girls continue developing through their teenage years, and even women in their twenties notice changes in their shape, filling out and rounding. Boys may not get hair on their chest until they're college age (See also Human Sexuality).

The bigger issue to consider is that measurements and appearance don't make up a person. There is a lot more to you than what meets the eye, and although appearances do count in our looks-conscious society, they are not what really matters. Don't fall into the trap of equating your looks with your true self—"I'm a bad person because I'm not cute" or "I'm a good person because I am cute." A dazzling smile or a pert nose has nothing to do with your value as a human being. Take pride in being well groomed, but work most on the inner you—a kind heart, a clear mind, and a strong soul.

Growing pains—this is a time to focus on your strong points and ignore your weak points.

If you are alone and choking on something, try either or both of these techniques. Press your fist into your abdomen with a quick upward thrust. You may need to do this several times to expel the object. Or use the edge of a fixed object (like a heavy table) instead of your fist. Press your abdomen firmly over the edge of the table, chair, sink, or other nearby object.

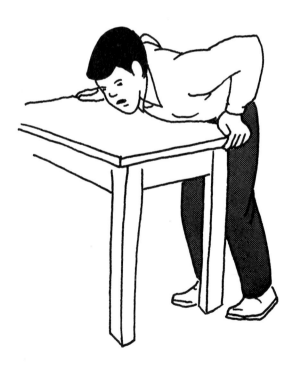

he Bare Bones Basics of First Aid

Heimlich Maneuver

An obstruction in the airway of the throat by a piece of food or anything else is an emergency. Sometimes the airway is only partially obstructed, and the victim can breathe enough to cough up the object. If so, leave him or her alone to do that. If the person is turning a bluish color and clutching the throat, he or she is most likely completely unable to breathe and needs your help. Before you begin the following procedure, check inside the person's mouth to make sure the obstruction isn't in the upper airway. If it is, you may be able to use your finger to dislodge it.

1. Stand behind the victim, slightly off to one side. Lean him or her forward a bit, supporting him or her with one hand. With the heel of the other hand, give the victim four hard thumps between his or her shoulder blades. (The victim can be standing or sitting while you do this.)

2. If the above doesn't dislodge the trapped object, wrap your arms around the victim's waist. Both of you should be in a standing position, with you behind the victim. Place one fist (thumb in) at his or her belt line and your other hand over the fist. Quickly thrust hard in and up toward his chest.

3. This abdominal thrust should do the trick by forcing air back up the airway, which in turn forces the trapped object out. If the abdominal thrust doesn't work, repeat it three times. Then, if the obstruction is still there and the victim has lost consciousness, turn him toward you, and repeat four more back blows. Once the obstruction is dislodged, if the victim still is not conscious, give him or her mouth-to-mouth resuscitation by: a) lying the victim down, b) tilting his or her head back and supporting the neck with one hand, c) using your other hand to pinch the victim's nostrils closed, and d) taking a deep breath, placing your mouth tightly over his or her mouth, and giving four quick breaths, one breath every five seconds. Keep an eye on the victim's chest to see if it is rising, and place your ear over his mouth when you inhale to hear if he or she is resuming breathing.

Your Digestive System and Intestines

Stomach Ups and Downs

The food processing plant in your stomach is an amazingly efficient system. But it is also a delicate one. It can be upset by the food you put into it, by the liquids you drink, by your emotions, and even by the air you breathe. It has strong likes and dislikes, and it lets you know what it does not like by burning, churning, growling, and sometimes sending back up what you put into it.

As we get older our digestive system works less efficiently. But at your age, the main culprit of stomach problems is usually your emotions. How can what you feel in your heart and think in your head make your stomach hurt? Emotions can stimulate acids in your stomach to work overtime. The way you're feeling emotionally can also affect the way you eat, which in turn affects the way your stomach feels. It is a fact that people who have ulcers tend to be people who hold in feelings that bother them to excess or let them out frequently in the form of rage.

If you've been having stomach problems lately, give some thought to whether it could be the tacos you've been eating every day for lunch or whether it might be something more complex. Are you worried? Are you feeling anxious? Try to figure out whether your ailments can be helped by a simple change in diet or by understanding your worries and trying to set them at ease. (See also Nutrition.)

Your digestive system begins in your mouth. Your teeth and tongue break down—or masticate—food and your salivary glands break it down further with liquid enzymes. As you swallow, the food travels through your esophagus to your stomach and on to the duodenum, the first section of the small intestine and a very important part of the digestive process. Your liver and pancreas secrete substances that further break down food into separate parts, such as fat and sugar. The large intestine serves mainly to absorb water and remove waste to be passed out of your body through your rectum and then anus and urethra (not shown).

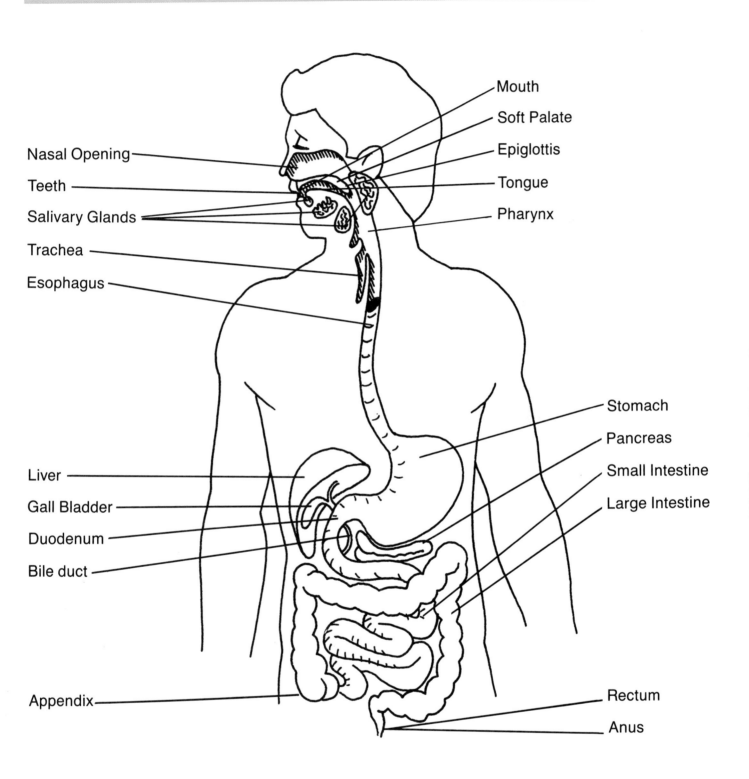

Nasal Opening

Teeth

Salivary Glands

Trachea

Esophagus

Liver

Gall Bladder

Duodenum

Bile duct

Appendix

Mouth

Soft Palate

Epiglottis

Tongue

Pharynx

Stomach

Pancreas

Small Intestine

Large Intestine

Rectum

Anus

Poison Safety

By now, you're old enough to recognize what is poisonous and what is not, but your four-year-old brother or the three-year-old you babysit for is not. Here are some dangerous situations or habits that you should watch out for in your home or in the home of the people for whom you babysit—they could lead to an accidental poisoning.

○ You tell your little brother that chewable vitamins are "candy." He could eat the whole bottle someday!

○ Cleaning products are stored on counter tops and window ledges, on the floor or a bottom shelf, or in a low cabinet without a safety latch. Move them out of reach of a curious child.

○ Toilet bowl cleanser is kept behind the toilet on the floor, and tub cleanser is kept on the bathtub ledge. Move them into a high cupboard out of the reach of a child.

○ Your mom keeps her prescription drugs in the kitchen so she'll remember to take them, then takes one whenever she's in the kitchen and it's time for a dose. You little sister may think that the pills are a treat and try to copy your mom.

When you are home alone with your little brother or sister or when you are babysitting, make sure that the number for the poison center in your area is near the phone. If you have to call them with an emergency, be sure to tell them these things:

○ The age of the person who was poisoned

○ The physical condition of the person (vomiting, passed out, etc.)

○ The name or description of the product the person took

○ The amount of time that has passed since the person took the poisonous substance

○ The address where you are

Then listen carefully to the instructions the poison center gives you and follow them until someone comes to help.

he Bare Bones Basics of First Aid

Poisoning

Any solid, liquid, or gas substance that can be fatal or cause serious harm to your body when ingested is a poison. Of course, preventing poisoning is preferable to treating it—for example, keep poisonous cleansers out of reach of your baby sister or a child you're babysitting. But accidents happen. Here's how you can help if you know someone who's been poisoned.

- First, call a poison-control center (have the number of a local one near your phone). Many accidental poisonings can be treated at home, but get professional advice first.

- If the victim can be treated at home, the object is to dilute the poison in the victim's stomach and then get him to vomit it up as soon as possible, but *only if the poison is noncaustic (nonburning)*—for example, aspirin, barbiturates, poisonous plants. Give the victim one or two glasses of water and then a tablespoon of syrup of ipecac, something every household should have. Follow with another glass of water. The ipecac should induce vomiting within 15 or 20 minutes; if it doesn't, repeat the dosage once. If you have no syrup of ipecac, place two fingers on the tongue back toward the tonsils to gag the victim and induce vomiting.

- *If the poison is caustic (acid),* for example, ammonia, toilet bowl cleanser, bleach, lye, automatic dishwashing products, kerosene, gasoline, or turpentine, *do not induce vomiting.* Corrosive substances do more harm coming back up than they do remaining in the stomach. Instead, unless you've been told otherwise by a doctor or poison-control center, dilute the poison in the victim's stomach with milk, milk of magnesia, or an over-the-counter antidote that contains activated charcoal, which absorbs the chemicals in the poison and acts as a buffer in the stomach. Take the victim to the nearest doctor or poison control center.

- *If the poison has been inhaled* in the form of oven gas or other toxic fumes, simply get the victim outside into fresh air immediately.

Your Reproductive Organs and Hips

Puzzling Puberty

For at least the first ten years of your life, not much happened below your waist. When you were little, your mother taught you how to take care of yourself when you urinated and had bowel movements, and there wasn't much else to think about.

Now all of a sudden there's a lot going on down there and a lot to think about. Your body is producing sperm or eggs that have the potential for creating human life. This is a pretty amazing transformation, so it's not surprising that you can see some of the changes taking place, as well as feel them. You now have pubic hair around and on your genitals. Your body is growing and filling out in many places. If you're a girl, your hips are spreading and getting rounder. If you're a boy, your penis is getting hard and stiff at times. You

may be experiencing sensations you've never felt before. You may be more interested in the opposite sex than you've ever been before. These are perfectly normal feelings (see Human Sexuality), and there's no reason to feel ashamed of them.

But this doesn't mean you should act on these feelings, however. Rushing into having sexual relations with another person is something you can't take back and may deeply regret. Nervousness, immaturity, not being in love with your partner, and not feeling comfortable contribute to bad first sexual experiences.

You shouldn't feel ashamed or believe any adult who calls you evil or bad for being curious about sex. You're not. More likely, the adult who tells you this has the sexual problem. It's normal to touch your body and try to understand how it's changing. If you're a boy, it's normal to have "wet dreams"—sexual dreams or thoughts that occur while you sleep and cause your penis to harden, become erect, and ejaculate sperm. In your struggle to understand yourself and your body better, there is hardly anything that is abnormal.

GIRLS . . . . . Avoid vaginal infections by being sure to always wipe yourself after a bowel movement from front to back, not the reverse.

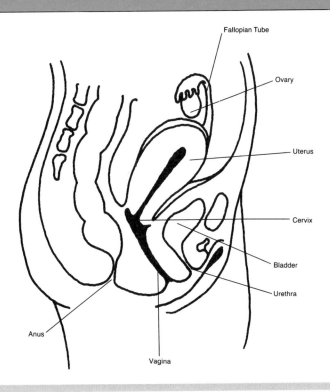

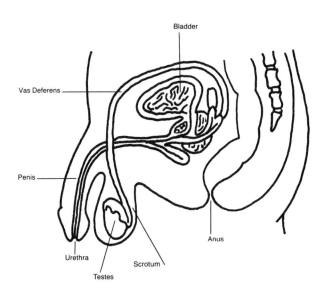

BOYS. . . . Check your testicles periodically (the best time is after a hot bath or shower, when the scrotum is most relaxed) by placing your index and middle fingers under each testicle and your thumb on top and rolling the testicle between your thumb and fingers.

ips In and Out of Fashion

These days, most girls will be happy to learn, hips are back in style. But fashion is only constant in being fickle, and, over the years, women's hips have been in and out of style. Considering that there is a physiological need for women's hips to be wider than men's hips, it seems silly that they'd be at the mercy of the whims of fashion—if women's hips and pelvises were as narrow as men's, getting babies out of the birth canal would be very tricky. Nevertheless, hips have been and continue to be viewed according to the styles of the times. And certain people have made a big impact on what those styles were. Here are a few worth noting.

○ *Flappers of the 1920s* popularized the no-hips look by starving themselves to boy-like proportions. They were also known to wrap their bosoms to obtain a flatter look. Flat chests and no hips, you see, looked best in the narrow chemise-style dress of the day that the designers decided women should wear.

○ *Sweater Girls of the 1930s and 40s* brought shapely hips back into style. After a decade of women trying to look like boys, the opposite style was embraced enthusiastically. Women were probably just as sick of trying *not* to look like women as men were of looking at them this way.

○ *Marilyn Monroe and Elvis Presley*—a beautiful, blond, curvy woman was no surprise as a hips trendsetter, but nobody expected a young man who played wild guitar to influence what people thought about hips. With his pelvic bumping-and-grinding dance style, Elvis did just that.

○ *Twiggy* set hipstyles back 40 years with her curve-less, emaciated body. Women dieted, starved themselves, flogged their rounded hips, and bemoaned the fact that they would never look like a "twig."

○ *Christie Brinkley* got hipstyles out of the 1960s and into the healthy, womanly style of the 1980s by making feminine hips look good again. Girls and women everywhere heave a sigh of relief—it's OK to have hips again. Let's hope this style lasts.

Your Legs, Ankles, and Feet

Give Your Legs a Break!

Your lower limbs take an awful lot of abuse and still keep you walking around. Holding the rest of your body up, carrying you around as you pound along hard pavement, your legs and feet rarely get a break—some days not until you go to bed. In your leisure time, you may demand more of your legs than you do during the normal course of the day by taking part in some kind of weight-bearing exercises such as running, playing basketball, football, baseball, soccer, hockey, and tennis. This type of exercise *is* good, but it's hard on your legs and feet and can be damaging to your ankles too.

You need to balance the weight-bearing exercises you do with exercises that stretch and relax your leg muscles (see Exercise). One of the best ways to do this is with yoga. Many devotees of yoga are involved in it for religious and spiritual as well as physical reasons. But at the center of its physical philosophy is something called "yin and yang." This means that for every movement you do, there is an opposite and complementary movement to follow it. So, when you arch your back with your head reaching backward for your toes, you follow this exercise with one in which you round your back, stretching like a cat.

The idea of complementary opposites is simple and you can apply it to your exercise program even if you have no interest in yoga. If you lift weights three times a week, do slow stretching exercises on the alternate days. If you play basketball several times a week, try to get some swimming time in to relieve your legs and feet of the pounding they take on the court. In fact, because swimming exercises your body and your heart without putting any stress on your joints, it's a great way to workout in general. The weightless feeling it provides makes it relaxing.

Vary your physical activity routines, wear shoes that give your legs good support, stretch for every time you tense your muscles, and your legs, ankles, and feet will probably return the favor by keeping you mobile.

© Steve Smith/Wheeler Pictures

he Right Way to Clip Toenails

Do—clip straight across and file edges straight across too.

Don't—clip into the sides of nails because it can lead to uncomfortable ingrown toenails, which are nails that grow too deeply into the corners of your toes.

If—you get an ingrown toenail, clip a tiny V-shape into the center of your nail to encourage the sides of your nail to "fill in" the V and grow out quicker.

© Michael A. Keller/FPG International

isten to Your Body

Most of the time your body knows exactly how to maintain itself, but it needs you to do some of the actual caring. Pay attention to the signals your body gives out ("I need food," "I need rest," "I need exercise," "I need a doctor," "I need quiet"). Help your body care for itself by listening to these cues everyday, and then once a week do a thorough head-to-toe checkup on your physical and mental health: "How do I feel mentally?" "Is anything bothering me emotionally?," "Did that food I ate last night feel good in my body?," "Did I overdo it with exercise the other day?" Be prepared to do something about the answers that require action.

Get Well, Stay Well

Even the healthiest people get sick sometimes. We are all susceptible to colds, sore throats, sprained ankles, and bee stings. Short of living in antiseptic bubbles, all we can do is try to cut down our chances of becoming ill or injured. We can also learn how to care for ourselves when we do have a minor illness or injury. In this section of the book you will read about what causes certain health problems, what their symptoms are, and what you can do to help yourself feel better.

The Common (and Contagious) Cold

Also called an upper respiratory infection (URI), the cold is caused by any one of more than a hundred microorganisms known as *rhinoviruses* —in other words, germs. If you're a person of average good health, you may catch—pick up from someone already infected—a cold three or four times a year. Most colds last from three days to a week, and while most are not serious, they *are* annoying. Runny nose, sneezing, watery eyes, scratchy throat, coughing, and a heavy-head feeling are some of the typical symptoms of a cold.

○ Because a cold is a viral, not a bacterial, infection, antibiotics like penicillin have no effect on them. (Viral infections are caused by virus germs, and bacterial infections are caused by bacteria. Unlike viral infections, which usually affect many areas of your body at once—your head, nose, throat, and chest, for instance—bacterial infections often affect a localized area only—as in strep throat). There are scores of cold medicines on the market, but there is no cure for the common cold. Acetaminophen or aspirin plus cold medications can help you feel better while you wait for the cold to pass, but be sure to check with your doctor, parents, or another adult you trust before taking *any* medication. (Children and teenagers should not take aspirin when they have a fever from a cold or the flu because this combination has been linked to a serious disease called Reye's syndrome, which affects the brain, central nervous system, and liver.)

○ Rest, drinking lots of water and fresh juices (especially if you have a fever—a body temperature over 98.6°F), and a vaporizer or humidifier to keep air moist also help. Hot liquids such as clear (not creamy) soups and weak tea are good medicine because they're easy on your stomach and the steam that rises from them helps open stuffy sinus passages. Ice cream, milk, cheese, and other milk products aren't a good idea when you have a cold because they have the opposite effect of producing more mucus.

○ Doctors don't know whether vitamin C protects you from getting a cold, but some studies have shown that taking vitamin C at the first sign of a cold may help to make the cold less severe and to make it go away faster.

○ Your mother was right about chicken soup being good for a cold, but she was wrong about you catching a cold just by going outdoors with wet hair or getting your feet wet. These things may make you *feel* cold, but they don't give you a cold. On the other hand, not getting enough sleep or feeling depressed can lower your body's resistance to illnesses and make you more susceptible to a cold.

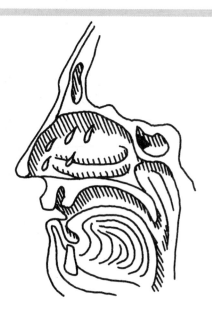

Oversecretion of mucus—otherwise known as a runny nose—is one of the more annoying and obvious signs of a cold.

The number-one way colds are spread is by hand—touching your hands to your eyes, nose, or mouth and allowing germs on your fingers to enter mucous membranes. Wash your hands frequently during the day, and try not to touch your eyes, nose, or mouth much. And, of course, be considerate of others by covering your mouth and nose when you cough or sneeze and then washing your hands.

© Joe McNally/Wheeler Pictures

Shot In the Arm

When you were a child, you probably felt that your parents were always taking you to the doctor to get a shot. Though you didn't understand it at the time, and you may not now, there are good reasons why your parents and the doctor subjected you to all that pain. In the past, a number of infectious diseases killed or seriously damaged many children and adults. Then doctors discovered that people could be protected against these diseases by immunization. The immunizing shot introduces antibodies—proteins that fight against a specific disease—into your body to combat the illness. Each of the shots you received contained a different antibody needed to ward off one of the deadly viruses.

Recently, some parents have neglected to have their children immunized. They believe that the worrisome diseases have been wiped out by widespread immunization. Yet it only takes one case of the disease to begin an epidemic among those not protected. Ask your parents or your doctor if you have received shots for the following diseases. If you haven't, check with your doctor about what you should do to protect yourself.

Polio Diphtheria Rubella
Tetanus Measles Mumps

The Ferocious Flu

Influenza, the full name for the flu, is also caused by a virus, usually type A or type B virus. There are many kinds of type A and type B viruses, however, and every few years a different variation appears somewhere in the world (there's been a Hong Kong flu, a London flu, etc.), often resulting in an epidemic. If you catch the flu (by coming into contact with an infected person's saliva when they sneeze, when you drink from their glass, or by not washing off germs that collect on your hands), you may at first think you have a cold. The early symptoms are similar, but they typically worsen to include fever, overall weakness, and muscle aches. For most of us the flu isn't a serious disease, but its symptoms can be severe, and recovery may take at least a couple of weeks.

○ The same treatments are recommended for the flu as for the cold. Although flu vaccines are available, they are generally given only to people in high-risk groups—those with heart disease, lung disorders, and elderly people.

Bed rest is the best treatment you can give yourself when you have the flu. Planning trips for when you get well doesn't hurt either.

What You Should Know About Commonly Used Medicines

Below is a list of some of the most widely used over-the-counter and prescription drugs. Most of these drugs are probably in your medicine cabinet right now. You've probably taken some of them when you've been ill. But how much do you really know about them? Read on, and find out.

An important note first: NEVER TAKE ANY MEDICATION WITHOUT YOUR DOCTOR'S OR PARENT'S ADVICE. ALWAYS READ AND FOLLOW DRUG PACKAGE DIRECTIONS CAREFULLY, AND CONTACT YOUR DOCTOR IMMEDIATELY IF YOU HAVE ANY SIDE EFFECTS. AS IS THE CASE WITH ALL DRUGS, INCLUDING ALCOHOL, THE FOLLOWING MEDICATIONS SHOULD BE AVOIDED DURING PREGNANCY UNLESS PRESCRIBED BY A DOCTOR.

Acetaminophen is often called an aspirin substitute or analgesic. It's used to reduce fever and relieve headaches and other kinds of pain; it also serves as an aspirin substitute in children and teens at risk for Reye's syndrome (see page 80, ''The Common (and Contagious) Cold'') and in people whose stomachs are upset by aspirin. Never take more than five dosages of acetaminophen a day and never take it for more than five days in a row.

Antacids are substances that balance out the acidity in your stomach and therefore relieve stomach pains. There are lots of antacid products on the market, but one of the most effective is ordinary sodium bicarbonate, or baking soda, diluted in a glass of water. Follow your doctor's directions for proportions.

Antibiotics are a group of powerful drugs that work to kill or severely inhibit the growth of bacteria. To be effective, however, they must be taken exactly according to your doctor's directions. You must continue to take antibiotics for as long as your doctor prescribes, even if you've begun to feel well before this time is up.

Antihistamines are drugs used to counteract or suppress allergic, or histaminic, reactions (e.g. sneezing, watery eyes, skin rashes, etc.). They are not effective against cold or flu symptoms because these are caused by an infection, not an allergy. A common side effect of this drug is drowsiness—*never* drive or operate machinery after you've taken an antihistamine. Some antihistamines are combined with other medications (such as acetaminophen) and are called cold remedies. Sometimes these can help you feel better; often they can't.

Aspirin is an *analgesic,* which means, pain reliever. It is used to reduce fever and inflammation, relieve headaches and other kinds of pain. It also has a mildly tranquilizing effect. Aspirin is one of the oldest and most dependable medicines, but it can cause stomach irritation in some people and lead to severe problems when used excessively. In recent years, it's also been found to cause a serious illness known as Reye's syndrome (see page 80) when taken by children and teenagers who are running a fever due to a viral infection, especially the flu or chickenpox. For this reason people under age eighteen should never take aspirin when they have a fever—acetaminophen should be used instead.

Cough Medicines have many names. Some are called antitussives (to suppress coughs), expectorants (to loosen mucus, or phlegm), and some are combinations of these two with added analgesics, decongestants (to clear nasal congestion), and antihistamines (to relieve allergy symptoms). Cough medicines containing codeine are very powerful drugs and should never be self-prescribed.

Ibuprofen is an anti-inflammatory analgesic, which means that it works by reducing inflammation. It is used to reduce swelling and fever, and pain that comes with arthritis, sprains, menstrual cramps, and headaches. People who are allergic to aspirin cannot take ibuprofen.

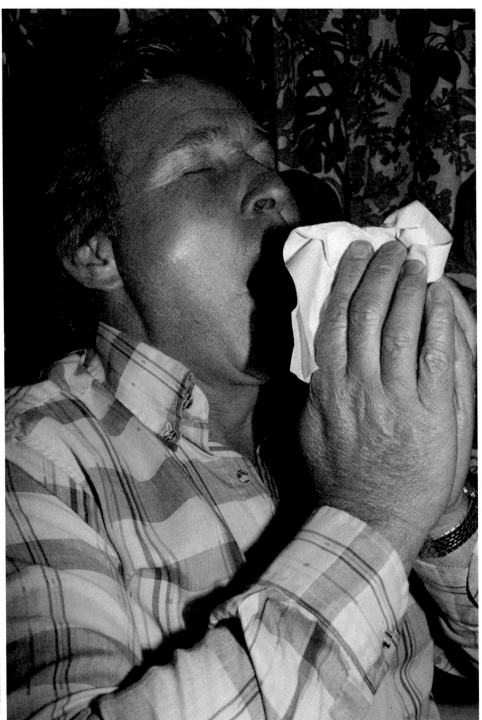

Why Do We Yawn, Sneeze, Hiccup?

○ *Yawning* is really just taking a deep breath with your mouth open. We yawn when we're tired, but we also yawn when we're not tired. If you're in a hot, stuffy classroom, your lungs may tell you to yawn as a way of taking in more oxygen and getting rid of the carbon dioxide that can build up in your blood. Next time you're in this situation, don't assume that your yawning is proof of how boring the subject matter is—instead, ask your teacher to open a window.

○ *Sneezing* is the body's way of dusting. When we sneeze, we clear bits of dust, hair, smoke, and even food out of the nose and trachea (throat). This is an important cleansing process, so you should never try to stifle a sneeze—doing so could cause sinus trouble, ringing in your ears, and also make blood vessels in your nose burst, resulting in a nose bleed. Let your sneezes out, but cover your nose and mouth as soon as you feel one coming on.

○ *Hiccuping* is the result of jerky movements in your diaphragm that create a clicking sound caused by the sudden, periodic closing of your vocal cords. They have been known to last for days, although they usually last only minutes or hours. Over the years people have concocted ways of curing themselves of hiccups—from standing on their head to getting someone to scare them. But the best methods seem to be holding your breath for a few seconds, slowing down your breathing, and slowly sipping a glass of water.

Stomach Aches and Pains

It can rumble, growl, flutter, bloat, and reject things you put in it. Your stomach has a variety of ways of expressing how it feels at any given moment, and how it feels can be the result of many factors. For example, being nervous can affect your stomach by affecting your digestive system. This is no surprise to anyone who's had a stomach ache before trying out for the basketball team—or any situation where the pressure's on.

When you're anxious about something, your nerves send out messages (called peristaltic waves) to the same glands and muscles that help your body digest food. Your mouth and stomach both get dry because your salivary and digestive glands stop working properly, and your stomach aches because your digestive muscles cramp. When you're relaxed and in pleasant surroundings, food usually goes down (and stays down) very nicely. (See also Stress and Mental Health and Nutrition.)

Here are antidote suggestions for various stomach ailments:

General Upset Stomach

The best medicine is prevention. Get into the habit of eating slowly, taking small bites, and don't drink ice-cold fluids with your meals if it seems to interfere with your digestive process. Also, be aware of which foods (spicy, creamy, fried, milk products) bother your stomach, and try to avoid them.

Vomiting

Vomiting can be a minor disturbance due to a virus, food poisoning, or a food that didn't "sit well," or it can be a symptom of a more serious problem. Taking an over-the-counter antidiarrheal or antinauseant medication can help control the vomiting, as can lying down with your head propped up slightly and your eyes closed. Bland, light foods (dry toast and weak tea) are usually best. If your nausea is caused by motion sickness, your doctor should be able to prescribe one of several medicines called antiemetics. If you know you're prone to motion sickness, don't read while in a moving car—it can trigger nausea.

Diarrhea

Diarrhea occurs when your feces (waste from your body) are watery and abundant. The main concern of diarrhea is preventing your body from becoming dehydrated or sapped of water. Antidiarrheals can curtail the problem, but you should consult your doctor before taking them, and try to figure out what caused your diarrhea. A common culprit is microorganisms in something you ate or drank. The key here is prevention. Microorganisms can be killed by cooking foods thoroughly and washing your hands before handling, cooking, or serving food. You also can avoid them by not drinking the water or eating unpeeled produce in places where there are poor sanitary conditions. Nervousness and food allergies can also cause diarrhea. While you have diarrhea, and for a few days afterward, replace the fluids you are losing by drinking lots of liquids, such as clear soups, fruit juice, tea, and ginger ale and eating foods that are easy on your stomach like puddings, crackers, and dry toast.

Constipation

Constipation is the exact opposite of diarrhea. It means having infrequent, difficult bowel movements in which your feces are hard and often dark colored. Laxatives relieve constipation, but they can be habit forming and dangerous. The best treatment is a natural one—eat more high-fiber foods and drink plenty of water every day. High-fiber foods, otherwise known as roughage, help bowel movements along by stimulating your digestive tract. (See Nutrition.)

Lactose Intolerance

This condition occurs when your body lacks an enzyme called lactase that is necessary for digesting lactose, a form of sugar found in milk and milk products such as ice cream and cheese. If you have lactose intolerance, you may experience stomach cramps, gas, and queasiness after drinking a glass of milk or eating a piece of cheesecake. If you have these symptoms, see your doctor. Once lactose intolerance has been diagnosed, the best way to prevent problems is to avoid eating milk products entirely or to eat them in small portions. You'll know what your body can handle.

Gas

Also called *flatulence,* gas is usually not cause for concern but can be cause for embarrassment. Avoiding gas-producing foods such as beans and other legumes and whole-grain breads and cereals usually helps reduce rectal gas. Unfortunately, these same foods are great for you in every other respect. Before you give up these foods altogether, try substituting different legumes and grains for the ones that seem to be making you gassy. Kidney beans in chili may give you gas, but split pea soup may not. Gas may also be caused by lactose intolerance.

How to Handle Minor Accidents and Incidents

Many of life's little accidents can be treated at home. Here are descriptions of some of the most common injuries and suggestions on what to do.

Bruises

What's black and blue and sore all over? A bruise, something that many of us live with on a fairly regular basis. A bruise is usually the result of a hard blow, or contusion, that causes blood vessels underneath the skin to break. The blood from those vessels then spreads out and "stains" the area. In various stages of your circulation, your blood is bluish, rather than the familiar red. This accounts for the coloring of a bruise. Right after you've suffered a blow, apply wet, cold compresses (wrap a washcloth around an ice cube, or run a cloth under cold water and ring it out) to the area for thirty minutes, or for as long as you can. The cold helps lessen the pain, swelling, and black-and-blue marks that will develop. It can take a few days to a few weeks for the blood stain under your skin to be reabsorbed by the sur-rounding blood vessels and for your bruise mark to disappear. (P.S.—If a friend or a child you baby-sit for has unexplained bruises on his or her body *a lot* of the time, tell a teacher, your parents, or any other adult you trust. This person could be an abuse victim, and you can help him or her by telling someone.)

Charley Horses

If you've ever had a charley horse, you know that it's a pretty light-hearted name for something that hurts so much. (Trivia: Ballplayers about 100 years ago are thought to be responsible for coin-ing this term after the name of a lame horse.) A charley horse is the pain you feel after a hard blow or squeeze on the front of your thigh. As with a bruise, blood vessels break and scatter blood beneath the skin; muscle, nerves, and tis-sues may also be slightly damaged. Apply an ice pack with pressure, and keep your leg elevated to help stop the internal bleeding. For the next couple of days, rest your leg as much as possible to speed healing. After two or three days, hot compresses or a heating pad can be used to im-prove circulation and hasten healing. If your charley horse is very painful, contact your doctor.

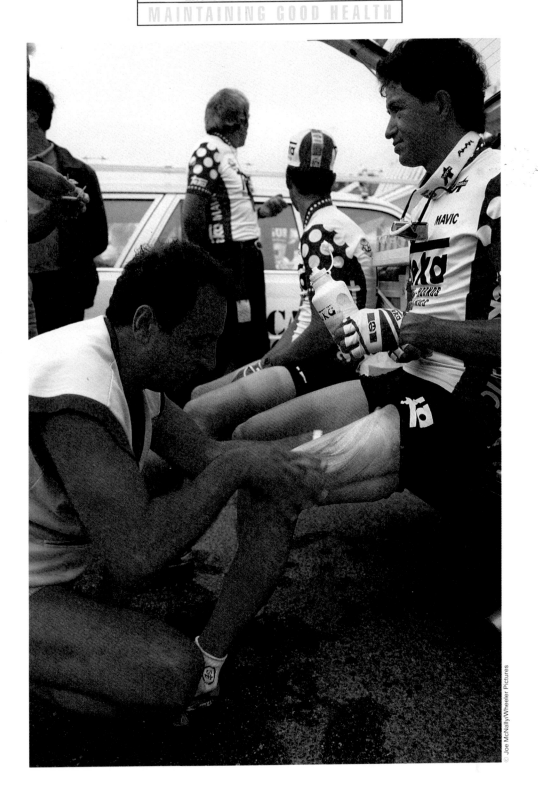

Muscle Cramps

If you're a runner, ballplayer, gymnast, dancer, bicyclist or even just an avid walker, you may have had the painful experience of waking up in the middle of the night with a muscle cramp. While you're asleep, cramps often occur in muscles that have worked hard (maybe too hard) during the day. Cramps may also occur while you're exercising or after bumping a tired muscle. Basically, muscle cramps are contractions—muscle fibers that normally alternate between resting and contracting when we are still, rapidly contract or tighten without alternately resting. You can try to avoid cramps by not overworking your muscles, by warming up with gentle exercises before strenuous activities, and by drinking water or juice before and after you exercise. When a cramp strikes, try stretching your muscle gently and massaging the area with firm pressure. It should subside after a few minutes.

Shinsplints

Shinsplints are another exercise-related injury, most often afflicting athletes who regularly run on a hard surface such as concrete. The pounding that your lower legs take when you run (or play tennis, basketball, etc.) is compounded when the floor or ground underneath is so hard that it doesn't absorb any of the shock, and, instead, your legs absorb it all. This causes the muscles in the front of your lower legs to partially separate from the bone, resulting in sometimes intense pain and swelling. If you develop shinsplints, see your doctor immediately. You can do a lot to avoid shinsplints by not running or exercising on hard surfaces, wearing athletic shoes that fit well and have good support and cushioning inside and on the soles, wearing an extra pair of socks for additional padding, and always warming up and stretching before exercising or participating in a sport.

If you suspect you have a dislocation, a fracture (broken bone), or any other serious injury, get medical attention immediately. (For more information, see Exercise.)

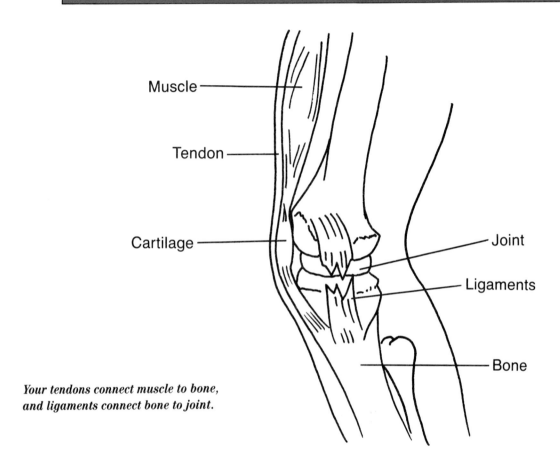

Muscle

Tendon

Cartilage

Joint

Ligaments

Bone

Your tendons connect muscle to bone, and ligaments connect bone to joint.

Sprains and Dislocations

Sometimes even when you do warm up properly and take sensible precautions, your body can take a strange turn or twist and you might end up with a painful sprain or dislocation. A sprain results when the ligaments or tendons—the tough fibers that act as connecting threads between two bones—are stretched or twisted too far. Blood vessels break and swelling occurs rapidly. The sprained area—most often ankles and wrists—should be wrapped firmly, but not so tightly that it interferes with your circulation. Ice packs should be applied for about fifteen minutes at a time, with fifteen-minute breaks between applications. If the sprain is very bad, see your doctor to make sure you have no broken bones. Dislocations occur when a bone is pushed out of its joint socket but is not broken. *Do not* allow anyone but a doctor to push the bone back into place. This is a very painful injury, and allowing someone who is well-meaning but unqualified to treat it can do you more harm.

Hazards of the Great Outdoors

Just being outside can put you at risk for many weather-related injuries. Luckily, with a little common sense, nearly all of these are preventable. (For more information, see Exercise.)

Hazards of the Cold

Hypothermia can hit a person who goes out into cold, damp weather unprotected or goes swimming in very cold water. Body temperature decreases, and he or she may become drowsy, have slurred speech, and have problems thinking clearly and moving easily. Exposure to extreme cold and wind can also result in frostbite. The affected parts of the body lose feeling, appear flushed and red, and then later appear pale and shiny. They often don't regain feeling for quite a while.

If you are swimming in cold water and begin to have the symptoms of hypothermia, do the survival or "dead-man's" float to regain energy to swim to land. Remove all wet clothing, wrap yourself in a warm blanket, and sip small amounts of a warm liquid—never alcohol. Then send for medical help. If you feel like you have frostbite, which often afflicts the extremities—toes, fingertips, nose—due to their limited blood circulation, go indoors and warm (do not *heat*) the frostbitten area gently and slowly with warm water baths or compresses. In the future, avoid cold-exposure injuries by wearing several layers of clothing rather than one thick layer. Keep all extremities covered, and remove perspiration- or rain-soaked garments.

Hazards of the Heat

Hot weather, too, has its hazards. Too much heat and sun can cause heatstroke, also known as sunstroke. Someone suffering from heatstroke will have hot, dry skin and a rapid, strong pulse. He or she should be moved inside to a cool, shady place and given cold-water tub or sponge baths, using cool, wet cloths or ice directly on skin. The victim may have convulsions or become unconscious, so it's important to call for medical help as soon as possible.

Heat exhaustion is another danger of hot weather. Usually it is the result of prolonged, strenuous exercise in very hot weather. It's caused by an excessive loss of bodily water and salt through perspiration. The breathing of someone with heat exhaustion is shallow, the pulse is weak, and the skin is pale and clammy to the touch. The victim should be moved to a cool place and given a salt-water solution (one teaspoon of salt in one quart of water) to sip slowly. Avoid heat exhaustion by replenishing the fluid you lose through perspiration with periodic glasses of water or juice and by not overdoing exercise in hot, humid weather.

Hazards of the Weather

Nobody ever really gets struck by lightning. Right? Wrong. They do, not in great numbers, but each year several hundred people are victims of lightning injuries, and a couple hundred die as a result. Your chances of being one of them aren't great, but in case you're ever caught outdoors during a thunderstorm, you should know how to keep yourself as safe as possible. Going indoors is the best protection against lightning—a car is good shelter because its rubber tires prevent it from being a conductor, or carrier, of electricity from the lightning. If you're in or near water, get out of it or move away from it—water is an excellent conductor of electricity. Although it seems like the right thing to do, do not stand under or near a tree, also a good conductor of electricity. If you're near or holding any metal objects—a bicycle, an umbrella, a fishing rod, railroad tracks, wire fences—drop them and/or move away. Metal is the best conductor of electricity. If you're in an open field or on a hill or mountain, try to make yourself as small a target as possible to minimize your chances of being struck, but *do not* lie on the ground. Crouch down, and bend forward. The smaller a target you are, the less likely you'll be one. If you are struck by lightning, get medical attention immediately.

Keep bees away by not wearing scented hair spray, deodorant, or perfume when you're going to be outdoors.

Hazards of Nature

For most people getting stung by a bee is just a momentarily painful experience. But for people who are allergic to the venom injected from a bee sting, it can be a life-threatening incident. Signs of sting allergies are: all-over or severe swelling, shortness of breath, wheezing, stomach pain, and faintness. If you know you're allergic to bee or other insect stings, there is a medicine kit your doctor can prescribe that you should carry with you when you're going to be outdoors in warm weather. The kit should include an antihistamine drug and premeasured doses of a medicine called epinephrine, which you inject into your skin after being stung. If you don't have this medication with you, or if you suspect your reaction to a sting is allergic, go to an emergency room immediately. In people with severe allergies to insect stings, death from a sting can occur within thirty minutes without medication.

You can avoid attracting bees and wasps by not wearing perfumes, scented deodorants, or hair sprays when you're going to be outside. If you're not allergic and are stung by a bee or wasp, check to see if the stinger—it looks like a splinter—is still in your skin. If so, gently draw it out (rather than pulling it out in one tug) to avoid releasing

© Dick Pietrzyk/FPG International

any more venom into your skin. Apply ice to the area to relieve pain and swelling and to minimize the spread of venom.

Shock

A serious danger of any injury, whether it takes place outdoors or indoors, is shock. Shock can occur after any injury, but most often in cases of extensive bleeding or burns. Shock means that the person's blood isn't circulating as it should, and it is a very serious condition in itself. A shock victim's breathing will be irregular, and his or her pulse will feel weak but fast (to check it, place two fingers at the person's throat or wrist). The victim's skin will look pale, or even bluish, and will feel cold and clammy. He or she may vomit, feel weak, or faint.

The first thing to do in a case of shock is to attempt to get the person's body temperature back to normal. Depending on the conditions, that may mean covering him or her with a blanket or providing shade from the sun. Try to control any bleeding with clean bandages and pressure to the wound. Lie the person down flat with feet slightly elevated, loosen his or her clothing, don't give anything to eat or drink, and don't move him or her any further. Get medical help immediately.

Cancer

Cancer is the second most common killer of people in this country (heart disease is number one). It can often be prevented by eating right (see Nutrition), not smoking, and limiting alcohol intake and sun exposure. You may know or be related to someone who has had cancer or died from it. Here are answers to some of the questions you may have concerning this disease.

Q. What is cancer?

Cancer is the name for a diverse group of different diseases that have one thing in common—*uncontrolled cell growth*. Cells are the components that are essential for making up the face, body, mind, and person we are. Cells normally grow and exist in an orderly pattern. However, in cancer cells, the growth and order are abnormal. When a doctor looks at cancerous cells through a microscope, he or she can actually see that they are oddly shaped and sized and that there are too many of them. Cancer cells form masses that are called tumors, and they rob "food" from healthy cells. If left untreated, they spread.

Q. Are all tumors cancerous?

The answer is no. Sometimes even healthy cells clump together and form a tumor. This is called a *benign tumor* (benign means not harmful). In this case the cells in the tumor are normal and grow in an orderly pattern. The tumor stays inside a wall of your tissue. It usually doesn't harm the rest of your body, though most doctors think even benign tumors are best removed.

A *malignant tumor* (malignant means evil or causing serious harm) is made up of cells that are abnormal and grow in an irregular pattern. Malignant tumors are a threat to your body because, unlike benign tumors, they can break through a wall of tissue and attack other parts of your body. This spread is called *metastasis*.

Q. Can cancer spreading be stopped?

Depending on the type of cancer it is and how advanced, or how much it has already spread, the cancer may be stopped through *surgery, chemotherapy,* or *radiation therapy,* or a combination of these.

When a tumor is in a part of the body that can be reached safely, a surgeon may be able to cut it

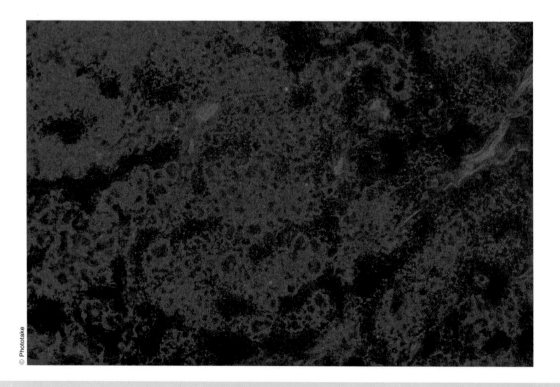

© Phototake

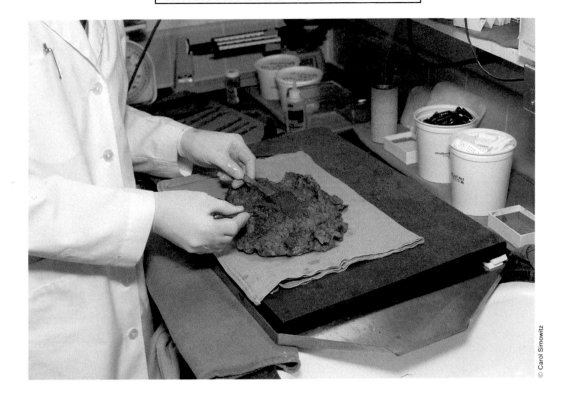

© Carol Simowitz

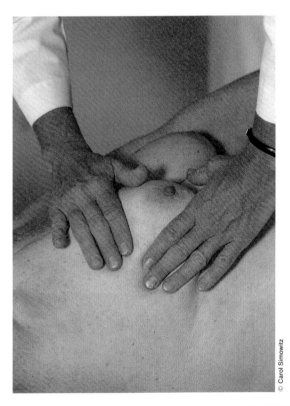

© Carol Simowitz

Above:
Tumors can grow very large within the body. Doctors have removed tumors the size of melons.

Left:
You should routinely perform breast exams on yourself. Press all around the breast area with the fingertips of both hands and gently squeeze nipples to feel for lumps.

Opposite page:
Cancer cells actually look different from normal cells. They are oddly shaped (often oblong instead of round) and irregularly sized.

out. In fact, doctors are now using a more effective tool than the traditional knife, laser beams, to do the cutting.

If the tumor can't be reached or if the cancer has spread to other parts of the body, chemotherapy or radiation may be used instead of or in conjunction with surgery. Chemotherapy involves using highly potent chemicals to kill the cancer cells. The drawback to this form of treatment is that it often has serious side effects on the patient. Radiation therapy, too, has side effects, but they are usually less severe—nausea, for example. In this therapy, different kinds and varying doses of radiation, which is an invisible and powerful form of atomic energy, are aimed at cancer sites in the hope of zapping the cancer cells enough so that they stop growing and even shrink. Cancer cells are very sensitive to radiation, more than normal cells are, but in this kind of therapy there is always the danger that healthy cells will also be harmed. In fact, radiologists (doctors who specialize in this therapy) have to be very careful because too much radiation misaimed can actually cause more cancer growth.

Q. Are these treatments cures for cancer?

Right now there is no cure for cancer. Surgery, chemotherapy, and radiation therapy are ways to try to stop or slow down the cancer. Like many diseases, both life-threatening and minor, the best "treatment" for cancer is prevention. Some cancers can't be prevented and some may even be inherited, but many can be avoided through careful living. What does that mean? It means reducing your risks by eating a healthful diet; not smoking; not drinking alcohol, or at least not excessively; maintaining a weight that's healthy for you; and by limiting or avoiding exposure to environmental carcinogens (things that cause cancer), such as polluted water. (This includes getting out of the way of someone else's cigarette smoke, or asking a person to not smoke around you—something you have a right and a responsibility to yourself to do.)

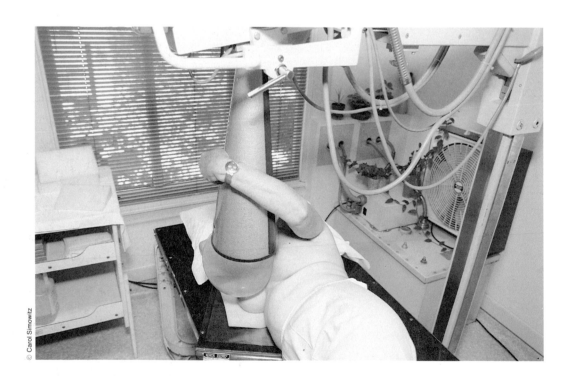

© Carol Simowitz

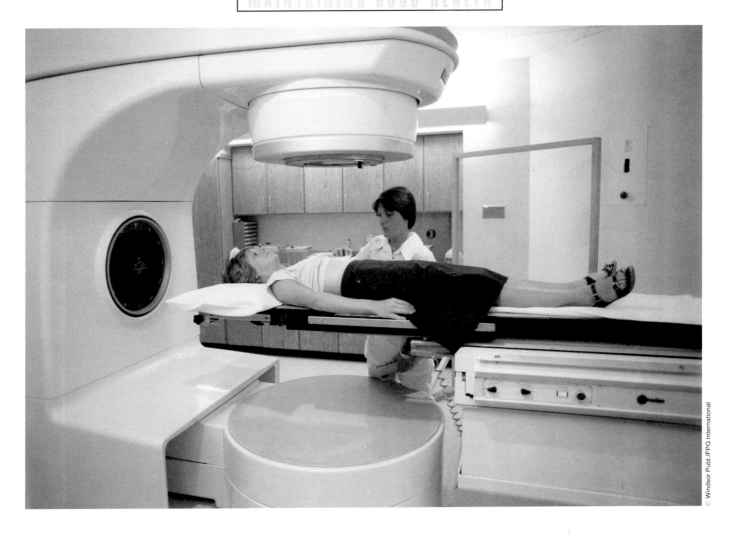

An oncologist is the name for a physician who specializes in the study and treatment of tumors.

Radiation therapy is used to treat cancer in the hope that it will arrest (stop) and even shrink cancerous cells.

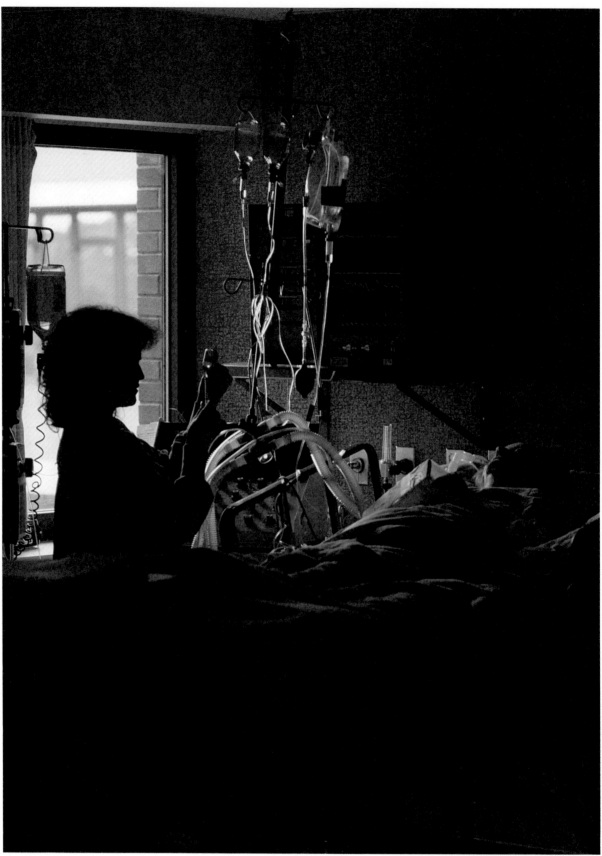

arning Signs of Cancer

Although some cancers cannot be prevented, and there is no cure for cancer, early detection of this disease goes a long way toward saving lives. If you or someone you know has any of the following warning signs of cancer, see your doctor or encourage him or her to see a doctor immediately.

- *Unusual bleeding or discharge* from anywhere in your body that can't be explained by menstruation, a wound, or any other "normal" situation.

- *A lump or thickening* in your breast or testicles or anywhere. This may be nothing more than a benign tumor or, less serious, a water-filled or fatty cyst, a clump of cells plus water or fat tissues that is not serious, but you need to find out immediately.

- *A sore that doesn't heal.* This can be a sign of skin cancer.

- *A change in bowel habits.* Any change from what is normal for you that lasts a few days should be checked. Persistant diarrhea, constipation, or change in stool size or color are examples of changes to have checked.

- *A cough or hoarseness that doesn't go away.* This could be a sign of throat or lung cancer, particularly if blood is spit up.

- *Persistant indigestion or difficulty swallowing* are early signs of cancers of the intestines and esophagus.

- *Any change in a mole or growth on your skin* should be checked for skin cancer.

- *A sudden, unexplained weight loss* often occurs as a result of several cancers; loss of appetite is another sign.

- *Unusual bruising* can be a sign of *leukemia,* a cancer of the blood.

- *Unexplained chronic (lasting) pain, especially in the bones.* Leukemia and bone cancer are often characterized by a deep, aching feeling in the bones and back.

- *Chronic fever* is usually a sign of infection and a weakened immune system, something cancer also brings about. Any fever that lasts more than a few days and cannot be explained should be checked.

© Dick Luria/FPG International

Stress and Cancer Connection

It's good to know the warning signs of cancer, but worrying excessively about whether you have any of them may actually have a bad effect on your health. (You've heard the saying, "she worried herself sick. . . .") Doctors are just beginning to study the role that stress plays in the development of certain cancers, although a link has been suspected for more than 100 years.

Stress, it seems, not only has the power to make us feel tense physically and mentally, but also to cause changes to occur in the cells that make up the body.

Unfortunately, we live in a stress filled world, and eliminating the sources of stress from our lives can be impossible. But what we can all do is change the way we respond to stress so that we don't become its victims. Instead of allowing ourselves to soak up stress like a sponge, we can train ourselves to become more immune to it. A few ways of doing this are: getting exercise each day; taking deep breaths at tense moments and learning how to meditate (see page 106, "Meditation"); maintaining a sense of humor about life; keeping in mind which things are *really* important and which are not worth getting upset over; and taking "time-out" breaks to do things you find relaxing, whether it's shooting hoops, listening to music, or washing your parents' car. If you want to know more, see Stress and Mental Health.

Warning Signs of Too Much Stress

- Irritability
- Pounding heart
- Hyperexcitedness or depression
- Vague or intangible anxiety
- Dry mouth
- Inability to concentrate on task at hand
- Insomnia or sudden need for lots of sleep
- Urge to cry, run away, hide
- Teeth grinding
- Impulsive behavior
- Dizziness or weakness
- Loss of appetite or undereating or overeating
- Increased sweating or urination
- Upset or queasy stomach
- Use of drugs, increased use of alcohol or cigarettes
- Nightmares
- Accident proneness

editation

A lot of people get scared off by the word meditation. It's really not as hokey as it sounds. Very simply, it is a way of calming down your body and mind to a level of relaxation that you may not even experience while you're sleeping. For those who practice it, meditation is a way of balancing the demands and stresses of everyday life, putting things in their proper perspective, and simply giving themselves a break from all of the stimuli they are bombarded with as soon as they open their eyes each morning. Meditation, it's been said, is the process of losing your mind to come to your senses.

There are many forms of meditation, some more religious and spiritual in origin, some more complex than others. Here are a few general steps to guide you in beginning a simple meditation routine:

1. Take off your shoes. Loosen your clothing. Dim the lights. Sit or lie down in a comfortable position. Make sure you'll have as few distractions as possible.

2. Close your eyes. Take a deep breath through your nose, make it fill your abdomen, not just your chest. Exhale through your nose. Be aware of how your abdomen rises and lowers as you inhale and exhale. In order to relax your body, your breathing should be slow, deliberate, and rhythmic. Take slightly deeper breaths each time you breathe, inhaling and exhaling as completely as you can. Fill your lungs from the bottom up. Picture your abdomen as a balloon filling and emptying with each breath. Concentrate on slowly letting go of the breath. Feel yourself relaxing, and be aware of what the air in your chest and lungs feels like. (This will make you realize how shallow your normal breathing is.) You might actually feel a little dizzy after a few minutes of breathing; don't worry, it's a good sign.

3. Repeat a word or sound in your mind, or out loud, as you exhale. Yoga meditators say "Om"; you could say "One" or anything else that you feel comfortable saying

and that works for you. Or, you don't have to say anything. Some people find it distracting, others feel it helps them focus on relaxing and keeps their mind off other things.

4. When you begin meditating, you may be distracted by other thoughts popping in and out of your mind. Don't worry about this; worrying will only make you concentrate more on the random thoughts instead of on meditation. People who've been meditating for years say that thoughts are like birds that fly back and forth over their head—you can't stop them from flying, but you can keep them from making a nest in your hair. Let your thoughts fly above you and go back to concentrating on your breathing.

5. Tense and then relax each of the muscles in your body, one at a time, beginning with your face, working your way down to your toes. If you've been sitting, it helps to lie down at this point. Notice the difference between the tensed and then relaxed muscle on each body part. Let your relaxed muscles sink into the floor. (If you try this exercise on one side of your body from head to toe and then on the other, you'll really see how much more relaxed the "exercised" side feels than the other.)

As you're meditating, don't allow yourself to fall into the trap of evaluating your performance. You are not performing. The goal is for you to adopt as passive an attitude as possible. Let the relaxation come to you, don't go chasing after it. If it doesn't come—and sometimes it won't—give up and try again later. Meditation cannot be forced. Try to practice these techniques once or twice every day for about 20 minutes. Morning and evening seem to be good times for many people, and it's usually advised not to try to meditate right after a meal because digestion interferes with the relaxation process. You can also do an abbreviated version of this 20-minute technique by sitting comfortably in a chair and just breathing deeply, inhaling and exhaling as fully and slowly as you can, for two or three minutes. It's a nice way to escape from daily pressures.

© Sandy Roessler/FPG International

Why Sleep Is Important

Did you know that you'll spend almost a third of your life sleeping? This might seem like a waste of time (though chances are, at this time of your life you love to sleep). On the contrary, sleep is such an important bodily function, and although it can be postponed and skimped on for awhile, if neglected for too long it will eventually take over.

Different things can cause changes in your normal sleep schedule and pattern. Excitement, boredom, emotional strain, exercise, alcohol and drugs, being overweight, poor diet, nervousness, and a change of environment can all affect your sleep for better or worse.

Sleeping Too Much

Teenagers are famous for sleeping a lot. Going through the process of growth does seem to make people need more sleep than usual. If you're requiring more sleep than you used to, don't be concerned—usually your body knows what it needs. But if you're sleeping so much that you're hardly functioning, think about the possibility that something deeper might be bothering you. Ask yourself whether you feel sad or depressed or anxious about something. Sleeping excessively can be a sign of depression. If you're concerned about this possibility, talk to your parents or a trusted teacher or other adult friend.

Sleeping Too Little

If you're having trouble getting to sleep or staying asleep, then you have the opposite problem—*insomnia*. For most people insomnia is an occasional annoyance, usually caused by a stressful change, tension, or even happy anticipation of a special day. Insomnia can also be caused by too much caffeine (found in cola drinks, tea, coffee, and chocolate), alcohol, or a heavy meal before bedtime. Even watching an exciting or frightening program on television can interfere with your sleep, as can napping during the day.

Physical activity during the day can cure insomnia by relaxing your body through exercise (but exercising right before bed can cause it by revving you up: see Exercise.) Getting out of bed and reading or doing some other quiet activity can lull you to sleep. And your grandmother's warm milk cure is based on scientific fact—milk contains an amino acid (the substance that produces protein in the body) called tryptophan that is converted to a sleep-enhancing compound in the brain. (See Nutrition.)

REM Sleep

The average person's eight hours of sleep a night are divided into two types of sleep: rapid-eye-movement, *REM* sleep, and non-REM sleep. During REM sleep, your eyes move around quickly under your closed lids, your heart rate increases, and all your automatic body processes speed up. These periods last about 20 minutes at a stretch and occur four or five times during the night. REM sleep alternates with non-REM sleep, during which your body functions slow down and you get your deepest sleep.

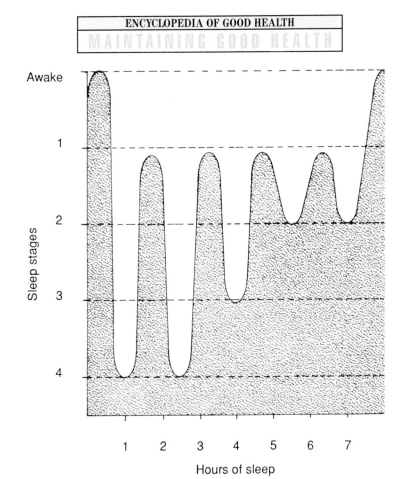

S *weet Dreams*

Doctors predict that you'll spend one third of your life asleep. Scientists still don't quite understand what function sleep serves, but they have been able to document the four stages of sleep. During stage one, your body and mind are relaxing, but you are not really unconscious. Many thoughts flit through your mind, and if you are awakened during this stage, you will probably feel as if you were never asleep. In stages two and three, your brain waves become considerably wider, and you have no conscious thoughts. If someone opened your eyes during these stages, you would not see. Stage four is the REM stage—the profound state of unconscious and the most fascinating and confusing stage of rest. Your eyes and mid-ears vibrate, your pulse quickens, and your brain temperature and blood flow increase. You have your most vivid and creative dreams during this stage.

Most people spend twenty to twenty-five percent of their sleep time in the REM stage. It takes about an hour for your mind to go into REM the first time, then you go in and out until you gradually return to consciousness.

GLOSSARY

Acetaminophen Aspirin substitute or analgesic, used to reduce fever and relieve pain.

Anabolic steroids Anti-inflammatory drugs made from synthetic male hormones, often abused by body builders and athletes to promote muscle bulk.

Antibiotics Powerful drugs that work to kill or stop the growth of bacteria in certain illnesses.

Autonomy The state of being independent and free to make one's own choices and decisions.

Cardiopulmonary resuscitation Also called CPR, a lifesaving technique that uses both artificial respiration and artificial circulation.

Caustic Capable of burning, corroding, or destroying living tissue; acidic.

Chemotherapy The use of highly potent chemicals to treat cancer and other diseases.

Contusion An injury, usually caused by a blow from a blunt object, in which blood vessels under the skin are broken but the surface of the skin is not damaged; a bruise.

Cyst A fluid-filled sac under the surface of the skin; may be filled with water or a fatty substance.

Decibel The unit used to measure the intensity of a sound wave.

Flatulence Also known as gas; the state of generating gas in the body, usually caused by food.

Flossing Using dental floss to remove food and bacteria from between teeth.

Frostbite Damage to skin and tissues caused by prolonged exposure to extreme cold.

Hair shaft The external cylindrical filament growing from the scalp and body.

Halitosis Bad breath, whether caused by food, tooth or gum disease, or internal illness.

Heatstroke Also known as sunstroke; extreme fatigue or illness caused by prolonged exposure to heat and sun.

Hyperopia Also known as farsightedness; better able to see at a distance rather than up close because the eyeball is too short from iris to retina.

Hypothermia Lowered body temperature caused by overexposure to cold and damp weather.

Ibuprofen An anti-inflammatory drug used to treat swelling, fever, sprains, arthritis, and menstrual cramps.

Intimacy Feeling closeness, affection, and caring for someone and their feeling the same for you.

Lactose intolerance An inability to properly digest lactose, a milk sugar, due to absence of the enzyme lactase.

Lice Tiny insects that live on hair, drawing blood from underneath the skin.

Mental health continuum A yardstick of mental and emotional wellness; at one end lies mental illness and at the opposite end lies optimal well-being.

GLOSSARY

Metasasis The spreading of a disease, such as cancer, from one part of the body to another.

Mucous The fluid secreted by the mucous membranes; an excess of mucous in the sinuses is usually associated with the common cold.

Myopia Also known as nearsightedness; better able to see things up close rather than at a distance because the eyeball is too long from iris to retina.

Oncologist A medical doctor who specializes in the study and treatment of tumors.

Ophthalmologist A medical doctor who specializes in the anatomy, functions, and diseases of the eye.

Ototoxic drugs Medications such as aspirin and certain antibiotics that can adversely affect the ears (oto = ear, toxic = poison).

Peristaltic waves The series of contractions that work to push food down to the stomach.

Radiation therapy The use of an invisible form of atomic energy to shrink or destroy cancer cells.

Rapid eye movement Also known as REM, the period of sleep during which the eyes move quickly under closed lids, the heart rate increases, and all automatic body processes speed up; REM sleep occurs in 20-minute periods about four or five times a night and alternates with the quieter, deeper non-REM sleep.

Seborrhea dermatitis Also known as dandruff, is a harmless but annoying condition in which the scalp is dry and flaky; can usually be controlled by dandruff shampoos.

Self-actualization Living up to one's fullest potential.

Self-image The picture of oneself, whether accurate or not, that one carries around in one's own mind.

Shinsplints A painful condition in which the muscles in the front lower legs partially separate from the bone; usually caused by running or exercising regularly on a hard surface.

Styptic pencil A crayonlike stick containing a substance that stops bleeding; often used for shaving cuts.

Syrup of ipecac A liquid medication that is used to induce vomiting in cases of poisonings by non-caustic agents.

Tinnitus A ringing, buzzing, or hissing sensation in the ears caused by excessive noise, a head injury, allergies, and ototoxic drugs.

Tryptophan An amino acid (the substance that produces protein in the body) that is converted to a sleep-enhancing compound in the brain; found naturally in cow's milk.

Tumor A group of cells that form a mass or lump; sometimes they are cancerous, usually they are harmless.

Ultraviolet rays Also known as UV rays, they are the harmful rays of the sun that cause the most skin damage.

Upper respiratory infection Also known as a URI and the common cold, it is caused by a virus and characterized by a runny nose, watery eyes, sneezing, coughing, and a sore throat.

USEFUL ADDRESSES AND FURTHER INFORMATION

AA
P.O. Box 459
Grand Central Station
New York, NY 10163

Al-Anon Family Group Headquarters
P.O. Box 182
New York, NY 10159

Alcohol, Drug Abuse, and Mental Health Administration
5600 Fishers Lane
Rockville, MD 20857

American Academy of Child and Adolescent Psychiatry/Public Information
3615 Wisconsin Avenue N.W.
Washington, D.C. 20016
For a free pamphlet, "Glossary of Mental Illnesses Affecting Teenagers," send a large self-addressed stamped envelope.

American Academy of Pediatrics
141 Northwest Point Road
Elk Grove Village, IL 60007
Contact for information on choosing a pediatrician (a doctor who specializes in treating people up to age 18) or for general information on pediatrics.

American Cancer Society
19 West 56th St.
New York, NY 10019

American College of Obstetricians and Gynecologists
600 Maryland Avenue S.W.
Washington, D.C. 20024
Contact for information on gynecological (having to do with a woman's body) and obstetrical treatments, problems, or questions and for recommendations of ob/gyns in your area.

American Heart Association
7320 Greenville Ave.
Dallas, TX 75231

American Lung Association
1740 Broadway
New York, NY 10019

American Social Health Association
260 Sheridan Avenue, Suite 307
Palo Alto, CA 94306

ASPO/Lamaze
1840 Wilson Boulevard
Suite 204
Arlington, VA 22201
Contact for information on childbirth, childbirth education, nutrition during pregnancy and breastfeeding, and for recommendations on childbirth educators in your area.

Carnegie Council on Adolescent Development
c/o Carnegie Corporation of New York
437 Madison Avenue
New York, NY 10022

Consumer Information Center General Services Administration
Washington, D.C. 20405
Contact for information regarding consumer services, products, treatment, and rights.

Council for Sex Information and Education
Box 72
Capitola, CA 95010

HELP
638 South Street
Philadelphia, PA 19147
"Youth to Help Youth"; maintains telephone counseling service, legal, psychological, medical, and referral services.

The Jackie Robinson Foundation (JRF)
80 Eighth Avenue
New York, NY 10011
Develops the leadership and achievement potential of minority and urban youth.

Just Say No Foundation
1777 N. California Boulevard
Suite 210
Walnut Creek, CA 94596
Young student clubs dedicated to combating drug abuse among children.

National Association of State Alcohol and Drug Abuse Directors
444 N. Capitol Street N.W.
Suite 530
Washington, D.C. 20001

National Clearinghouse for Alcohol Information
P.O. Box 2345
Rockville, MD 20852

National Clearinghouse for Drug Abuse Information
P.O. Box 416
Department DQ
Kensington, MD 20795

National Clearinghouse for Smoking and Health
Westwood Towers, Room 500
5401 Westbard Avenue
Bethesda, MD 20016

National Council on Alcoholism
12 W. 21st Street
New York, NY 10010

National Family Planning and Reproductive Health Association
122 C Street N.W.
Suite 380
Washington, D.C. 20001

National Institute on Drug Abuse
11400 Rockville Pike
Room 110
Rockville, MD 20852

National Mental Health Association
1021 Prince Street
Alexandria, VA 22314
For a small fee, this organization will send you the pamphlet, "Adolescent Depression."

Network International
99 Hudson Street, 10th Floor
New York, NY 10013
Designs and organizes youth programs: i.e., City Kids Coalition, City Kids Speak.

Office on Smoking and Health Technical Information Center
Park Building, Room 116
5600 Fishers Lane
Rockville, MD 20857

Planned Parenthood Federation of America
810 Seventh Avenue
New York, NY 10019

Sex Information and Education Council of the United States
80 Fifth Avenue, Suite 801
New York, NY 10011

Students Against Driving Drunk (SADD)
P.O. Box 800
Marlboro, MA 01752

Target—Helping Students Cope with Alcohol and Drugs
P.O. Box 20626
11724 Plaza Circle
Kansas City, MO 64195
A project of the National Federation of State High School Associations. This is a resource center that provides information on chemical abuse and prevention.

INDEX

Muscles
  cramps, 92
  development, 58
  sprains, 93
Myopia, 43

N

Nature, hazards of, 96-97
Neck, 56
Needs, 17-18
Nervous breakdowns, 14
Neuroasthenia, 14
Noise, 49-50
Nose, 46-47
  sneezing, 87
Nosebleeds, first aid, 47

O

Olfactory nerve, 46
Oncologists, 101
Opthalmologists, 44

P

Palmistry, 60-61
Penis, 72
Perfumes, 96
Periodontal disease, 54
Perspiration, 59
Physical appearance, 65
Pimples, 30-31
Plaque, 53
Poison, 70
  first aid, 71
Posture, 56
Presley, Elvis, 75
Psychiatrists and
    psychologists, 14
Puberty, 72

R

Radiation therapy, 98-100
Realistic thinking, 15-17
Reproductive system, 72-73
Responsibility, 18-19
Reye's syndrome, 80, 84

S

Scalp, 29
Schizophrenia, 14
Sebaceous glands, 30
Seborrhea dermatitis, 29
Self-image, 19-20

Sexuality, 72
Shampoo, 25-26
Shaving, 34
Shinsplints, 92
Shock, 97
Silence, 20
Skin, 30-31
  burns, 41
  cleaning, 32-33
  picking at, 35
  shaving, 34
  stress and, 30, 36
  sun's effect on, 37-39
  treatments for, 32-33
  wounds, 42
Sleep, 108-9
Smell, 46
Smoking, 62-63
Sneezing, 87
Sodium bicarbonate, 84
Solitude, 20
Steroids, 58
Stomach, ailments of, 88-89
Stress
  cancer and, 104
  insomnia and, 108
  skin problems and, 30, 36
  warning signs, 105
Sun, skin, and, 37-39
Sunstroke, 95
Surgery, for cancer, 98-100

T

Teeth
  bad breath, 54
  brushing, 53
  cavities, 54
  flossing, 53
Throat, choking, 66-67
Tinnitus, 49
Toenails, clipping, 77
Tryptophan, 108
Tumors. *See* Cancer
Twiggy, 75

U

Ulcers, 68
Upper respiratory infection,
  80-81

V

Vaginal infections, 73
Vitamin C, 80
Vomiting, 88

W

Weather, hazards of, 95
Weight training, 58

Y

Yawning, 87
Yoga, 76